Word for Windows™ 6 Quick Reference

Que Quick Reference Series

Rich Grace

Library of Congress Catalog No.: 93-84124

ISBN: 1-56529-468-8

96 95 94   4 3

Interpretation of the printing code: the rightmost double-digit number is the year of the book's printing; the rightmost single-digit number, the number of the book's printing. For example, a printing code of 93-1 shows that the first printing of the book occurred in 1993.

Composed in *Cheltenham* and *MCPdigital* by Que Corporation

Screen reproductions in this book were created with Collage Plus from Inner Media, Inc., Hollis, NH.

Publisher
David P. Ewing

Publishing Manager
Charles O. Stewart, III

Product Director
Elden Nelson

Production Editor
Elsa Bell

Editor
Linda Seifert

Technical Editor
Michael Watson

Book Designer
Amy Peppler-Adams

Production Team
Jeff Baker, Angela Bannan, Laurie Casey, Michelle Greenwalt, Carla Hall, Bob LaRoche, Tina Trettin

Table of Contents

Introduction

Word for Windows 6 Quick Reference is a collection of the
most essential commands and functions available in
Word for Windows 6, assembled in a task-oriented quick-
reference format. Use this book to learn specific procedures as you learn the program itself. Keep the book
handy to refresh your memory on how to perform tasks
you need to carry out only infrequently.

Each reference entry in the Task Reference presents
information in the same format. A brief introductory
paragraph summarizes the purpose of the command.
Then step-by-step instructions explain how to use the
command. Within *Lists*, for example, you can find
information on creating numbered or bulleted lists and
on editing lists. Some entries also have tips, reminders,
cautions, and shortcuts to help you avoid errors and to
show you alternative ways to accomplish the tasks.

If you are new to the Windows environment, begin by
becoming familiar with the Windows features described
in *A Word for Windows Overview*. For more detailed
information about Windows 3.1, see Que's *Using
Windows 3.1*, Special Edition.

Word for Windows 6 Quick Reference is not intended to
replace comprehensive documentation. The book is
more like an abridged dictionary of common procedures. Que's *Using Word Version 6 for Windows*, Special
Edition, and *Word for Windows 6 QuickStart* are good
choices to add to your computer library for more
detailed instructions.

Hints for Using This Book

Word for Windows 6 Quick Reference shows you how to perform necessary word processing tasks with step-by-step instructions for those procedures. To get the most out of this book, first take time to read the overview section and to familiarize yourself with the new version of the program. Then turn to the Task Reference section to learn a specific task. Tasks are alphabetically arranged for easy reference. Each topic contains a brief explanation of its purpose, followed by instructions. Alternative methods of performing tasks are provided if applicable.

As you read this book, keep in mind the following conventions:

- Keys you press, text you type, and letters that are underlined on-screen (in menu names, commands, and dialog box options) appear in **boldface** type.

- Remember that to select a menu or a dialog box option, you hold down Alt as you press the underlined letter.

- When you see two keys separated by a plus sign (a "key combination" such as Shift+F7), you hold down the first key, such as Alt or Shift, as you press the second key.

- When you see two keys separated by a comma, you press and release the first key and then press and release the second key.

- Screen displays and messages appear in a special typeface.

- This book is extensively cross-referenced. For more information about a command or function, see the entries referenced in *italic* type.

A Word for Windows Overview

Word for Windows 6 is the premier word processor for document creation. It contains all the features you may ever need to create, format, lay out, and enhance traditional word processing documents.

Word for Windows 6 provides all the excellent word processing features that Word users have come to expect, and adds many new features.

The following table summarizes the new features of Word for Windows:

New Feature	Use
Auto Correct	Word for Windows can automatically correct minor typing errors such as **teh** for **the**, **adn** for **and**, **abotu** for **about**, and more.
Multi-level Dialogs	Many dialog boxes now offer multiple levels of functionality with the "File Tab" motif. Some dialog boxes (not all) will stay on-screen while you handle other tasks, such as basic text edits and selections.
Captions	Captions can be added to tables, illustrations, equations, and other objects. You can add captions automatically. They can also be formatted with styles and specially numbered, and updated automatically.

continues

New Feature	Use
Character Styles	New Font menu option allows more straightforward character formatting with additional character spacing specifications. Improved character spacing and pair kerning are also offered. (Pair Kerning is the process of setting the amount of space between special letter pairs such as "A" and "V," or "A" and "W," and so on.)
Cross-Referencing	Cross-references to Heading numbers, Page numbers, Bookmarks, Footnotes, illustrations, and more are available.
Drawing	Greatly enhanced drawing features include color fills, rotation of graphics, freeform polygon drawing, and custom callouts for drawings and illustrations.
Drop Caps	This typographic feature allows the first character of a chapter or paragraph to be enlarged and "dropped" for a classic chapter heading effect. Words can also be dropped.
Envelopes	Envelopes and label creation and printing have been improved.
Full Screen View	This feature provides a scrollable full screen display, eliminating the Word for Windows screen elements.

New Feature	Use
Grammar checker	You can proofread documents for correct grammar and language use.
Go To	The improved Go To feature enables you to go to a specified page, annotation, footnote, bookmark, line, table, and much more.
Help	This feature provides on-line, context-sensitive help for any function. Help includes an Index, "Getting Started" beginner's lessons, "Learning Word" advanced lessons, and WordPerfect Help.
Mail Merge	Enhanced Mail Merge capabilities include legal document assembly, faster data merging, a Mail Merge Helper, and easier use of existing documents for merging.
Multiple Undo/Redo	With this feature, you can recover mistakes made several actions back, and Redo actions in the same way.
Ruler	Improved ruler tools allow for easier indenting, tabs and margin setting, and visual handling. Hanging indents can be quickly set, and double-clicking on the Ruler also automatically allows you to bring up Page Setup and Tab dialog boxes for fast and precise formatting.

continues

New Feature	Use
Revisions	Improved revision handling includes revision marks, merging of revisions, and revision comparisons.
Save As	With this feature, you can save a file in another format or with another name.
Text Effects	Dozens of text effects such as bending, wrapping around curves, 3-Dimensional, and more are offered. You can save special effects and apply to other text.
Toolbars	Special toolbars for Drawing, Database, Microsoft applications links, Forms, and other functions are detachable and can "float" over the Word screen. You can create custom toolbars, and place every function in Word in a toolbar.
Tooltips	Toolbars also have a special feature called Tooltips, which provide a short description of each button's function on the toolbar as you pass the mouse over each button.
Tables	Word 6 offers support for more specialized table types such as Tables of Authorities for legal documents, and for Tables of Figures.

New Feature	Use
Workgroup Support	You also get support for document routing via E-Mail, network use of master documents, revision marks for denoting who has made changes in a document, annotation merging, revision tracking, and document protection.
Zoom	With this feature, you can enlarge or reduce the view of a page on-screen.

The Word for Windows Screen

When you start Word for Windows, the program appears in an *application window*. An application window includes a title bar, a menu bar, one or more toolbars, and the status bar.

When you open a new or existing Word for Windows document, the document appears in a *document window*. A document window includes a title bar, a Ruler, and horizontal and vertical scroll bars. Any of these elements can be displayed or not as the user chooses.

Title Bar

Located at the top of a window, the title bar displays the name of the application—in this case, Microsoft Word—the name of the user, and the name of the document.

Menu Bar

The menu bar, located directly below the application window's title bar, contains pull-down menus that list Word for Windows commands.

Toolbars

Toolbars, located directly below the menu bar, contain buttons for the most frequently used Word for Windows commands. You can display up to eight different toolbars, which offer many different functions with the click of a mouse. You may even create your own custom toolbars.

For example, the Formatting toolbar, located directly below the Standard toolbar in Word's default display, contains list boxes and buttons for formatting text. By selecting options on the formatting toolbar, you can change the style, font, point size, character formats, paragraph alignment, tab alignment, and the display of nonprinting characters (such as spaces, paragraph marks, and tabs) in a Word for Windows document.

Ruler

Located directly below the document window's title bar, the Ruler contains the document's tab and indent markers, margin markers, and boundaries for table columns. The Ruler enables you to format paragraphs, adjust margins, and change the width of table and newspaper-style columns for that document.

Scroll Bars

At the right side of each document window is a vertical scroll bar that contains an up arrow, a down arrow, and a scroll box. At the bottom of each document window, you will see a horizontal scroll bar that contains a left arrow, a right arrow, and a scroll box. Each arrow, when clicked on and held with the mouse, lets you scroll in the corresponding direction. Clicking and holding the down arrow scrolls down the document, for example.

Status Bar

The status bar, located at the bottom of the application window, contains information, indicators, and messages. The current page number, the section number, and the total number of pages in the document appear at the left end of the status bar. The insertion point's position in the document and the view magnification level appear in the center of the status bar. The Macro RECord, OVeRrtype, EXTended Select, and other Word for Windows indicators appear at the right end of the status bar.

The status bar also displays context-sensitive messages about the tools and functions you're pointing at with the mouse. If you're confused about a button on a toolbar, for example, the status bar will frequently tell you what the button in question is.

Using a Mouse

You can use a mouse with Word for Windows. In fact, Word for Windows is optimized for mouse use, so if you don't have one, buying a mouse might be a good idea. In fact, toolbars, one of the exceptional features of Word for Windows, are usable only with a mouse. You also can't perform drag-and-drop, an outstanding editing feature, without a mouse.

The following table describes the basic mouse actions you use in Word for Windows (or in any Windows program):

Mouse Action	Description
Point	Position the mouse pointer directly over the item that you will change or use
Click	Point to the item and then press and release the left mouse button one time.

continues

Mouse Action	Description
Double-click	Point to the item and then press and release the left mouse button two times in rapid succession.
Drag	Point to the item and then hold down the left mouse button as you slide the mouse across a surface (such as your desk).
Drag and Drop	Select the word, sentence, paragraph or block of text, and click and hold the mouse over the highlighted text. Move the insertion point to the place in the document where you want the dragged text to be placed, and release the mouse button.

Selecting Text

When you select, or highlight, text, you are defining a portion of text that you want to overtype, delete, move, copy, edit, or enhance. Word for Windows highlights text you select.

To select text by using the mouse

Place the mouse pointer at the beginning of the text you want to select, hold down the left mouse button, and drag the mouse pointer across the text you want to select.

To select a word, double-click the word.

To select a line of text, click the left margin next to the line of text.

To select a sentence, hold down Ctrl and click anywhere within the sentence.

To select a paragraph, double-click the left margin next to the paragraph, or triple-click the mouse anywhere inside the paragraph.

> **Tip**
>
> Sometimes, you'll double-click a word to select and drag it, and do the third click (and hold) for the drag operation too quickly. Then the entire paragraph will be unintentionally selected. To avoid this, pause briefly and then perform your third click and hold.

To select a block of text, position the mouse pointer at the beginning of the text you want to select, click the left mouse button, and then hold down Shift as you click the end of the block of text.

To deselect text by using the mouse

Click anywhere in the document outside the selected text.

To select text by using the keyboard

To select one character to the right of the insertion point, press Shift+right arrow.

To select one character to the left of the insertion point, press Shift+left arrow.

To select the line above the insertion point, press Shift+up arrow.

To select the line below the insertion point, press Shift+down arrow.

> **Tip**
>
> The last two line selections are best used with the insertion point at the beginning of the current line. If the insertion point is located somewhere in the middle of the line of text, all the text beyond the insertion point will also be selected in the direction you indicate.

To select text from the insertion point to the end of the line, press Shift+End.

To select text from the insertion point to the beginning of the line, press Shift+Home.

To deselect text by using the keyboard

Press any of the respective arrow keys.

To select text by using Extend mode

Extend mode is a method of quickly selecting blocks of text by using the keyboard or mouse. When Extend mode is turned on, the EXT indicator (shown as black letters) appears on the status bar at the bottom of the Word screen.

1 Position the insertion point at the beginning of the text you want to select.

2 Press F8 to turn on Extend mode. EXT will show on the status bar.

3 Press the appropriate arrow keys to move to the end of the text you want to select.

   To shrink the selection to the next smaller increment, press Shift+F8. The next smaller increment can be a word, line, or paragraph.

4 Press Esc to turn off Extend mode.

Choosing Menu Commands

A *menu* is a list of commands. In Windows programs, the menu names appear in the menu bar at the top of the screen. You can select menu commands by using the mouse or the keyboard.

To choose a menu command by using the mouse

1 Click the name of the menu that contains the command you want to select.

   Word for Windows displays that menu.

2 Click the command you want to select.

You can also drag the mouse pointer down the menu to highlight the command you want to select and then release the mouse button.

If you choose a command followed by an ellipsis (...), Word for Windows displays a dialog box from which you can choose additional options; otherwise, Word for Windows executes that command.

To choose a menu command by using the keyboard

1 Hold down Alt to activate the menu bar and type the underlined letter in the menu name. To select the Edit menu, for example, press Alt+E.

2 Press the underlined letter in the command name. To select **C**opy, for example, press C.

If you select a command followed by an ellipsis (...), Word for Windows displays a dialog box from which you can choose additional options; otherwise, Word for Windows executes that command.

> ## Reminder
>
> Letters underlined on-screen appear in **boldface** type in this book. When two keys are separated by a plus sign, you hold down the first key as you press the second key.

Selecting Dialog Box Options

Dialog boxes provide information, messages, options, and warnings associated with the functions you're trying to perform in the program.

When you select a dialog box button command followed by an ellipsis (...), Word for Windows displays a dialog box in which you supply additional information so that the command can execute.

Typing Information in a Text Box

A *text box* is a rectangular box where you type text or
other information. Text boxes normally appear inside
dialog boxes as an option you can select for entering
values or choosing from a list. To type information in
a text box, do one of the following:

- Click inside the text box and then type the
  information.

- Hold down Alt, press the underlined letter in the
  text box name, and then type in the information.

- Move to the text box by pressing tab or Shift+tab,
  and then type the information.

Selecting or Deselecting a Check Box

A *check box* is a small square box that appears next to
an option. When an option is selected (turned on), an X
appears in its check box. You can select more than one
check box from a set of options. To select or deselect an
option with a check box, do one of the following:

- Click the check box.

- Hold down Alt and then press the underlined letter
  in the option name.

- Move to the option by pressing tab or Shift+tab and
  then press space bar.

Selecting an Option Button

An *option button* is a small round button that appears
next to an option. When an option is selected (turned
on), a black dot appears in its option button. You can
select only one option button from each set of options.
To select or deselect an option with an option button,
do one of the following:

- Click the option button.

- Hold down Alt and then press the underlined letter
  in the option name.

- Move to that set of option buttons by pressing
  tab or Shift+tab and then press ↑ or ↓ to select
  the option.

Selecting an Option from a List Box

A *list box* is a small rectangular box that contains the name of the currently selected option and has an arrow at the end of the box. To select an option from a list box, do one of the following:

- Click the arrow at the end of the list box, drag the mouse pointer down the list to highlight the option, and then release the mouse button.

- Hold down Alt, press the underlined letter in the list box name, press ↑ or ↓ to highlight the option, and then press Enter.

- Move to the list box by pressing tab or Shift+tab, press the space bar to display the list, press ↑ or ↓ to highlight the option, and then press Enter.

A *drop-down list* is a rectangular box that contains a list of options and may have a scroll bar at the side of the box. To select an option from a drop-down list, do one of the following:

- Use the scroll bar to display the option you want to select and then click the option.

- Hold down Alt, press the underlined letter in the list box name, press ↑ or ↓ to highlight the option, and then press Enter.

- Move to the list box by pressing tab or Shift+tab, press ↑ or ↓ to highlight the option, and then press Enter.

Selecting a Command Button

A *command button* is an oblong button that executes a command in a dialog box. The most common command buttons are OK, Cancel, and Close. To select a command button, do one of the following:

- Click the command button.

- Hold down Alt and then press the underlined letter in the command button name.

- To accept your changes and close the dialog box, press Enter.

- To abandon your changes and close the dialog box, press Esc.

Moving a Dialog Box

You'll normally want to move a dialog box to have a better view of the screen behind it. It's an easy procedure, because you move dialog boxes just like any other window.

1 Click the title bar of the dialog box and hold down the mouse button.

2 Drag the dialog box to the new location and release the mouse button.

or

1 Press Alt+space bar to open the Control menu.

2 Press Enter to select the Move command.

3 Press →, ↓, ←, or ↑ to move the dialog box to the new location and then press Enter.

The File Folder Motif

Word for Windows 6 embraces a new method of providing additional levels of functions in a dialog box: the File Folder. For an example, choose Tools, Options. You see the following dialog box:

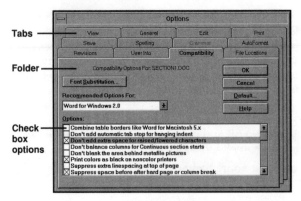

The Options dialog box features 12 "folders" that are tiled over one another, as if they were in a filing cabinet. When you click on the tab at the top of a folder, its contents come forward into view, changing the viewable contents of the dialog box. In any of the "folders," you can select or deselect check boxes, option buttons, and other typical dialog box elements. Folders are effective because many pull-down menu options are eliminated, which would otherwise present an extremely crowded menu.

Navigating Word Documents

You can open up to nine document windows and switch between the open documents by switching between their windows. You can move around a document window by using the mouse or the keyboard.

Opening New Documents

Whenever you need to create a new file in your word processor, you begin the process by opening up a new document. Each document you create has its own window, which can be moved, scaled, tiled, or mini-mized; you can perform any other typical Windows operation. You can use any of the following methods to open a new document:

- Choose the **F**ile menu with your mouse, and then choose the **N**ew command.

- Press Alt+F to choose the **F**ile menu and then press N to choose the **N**ew command.

- Click the New button on the Standard toolbar. (If you're not sure what it is, move the mouse over the dog-eared page icon in the toolbar. Keep an eye on the status bar to see a description of the function.)

To open an existing document, see *Open*.

Switching between documents

Switching between documents is a very straightforward process. It's often done when you're cutting and pasting text or pictures between documents, or when you need to do parallel edits in more than one document. To do so, choose the Window menu, and then choose the document to which you want to switch.

Moving around a Document

Using a mouse is often the easiest way to move around a Word for Windows document—simply click a different location on-screen or use the scroll bars to move to another area of the document.

You can use the mouse and the scroll bars to navigate a document in three ways:

- Click the up, down, left, or right scroll bar arrow to move up, down, left, or right in the document. If you hold down the mouse button, the document scrolls continuously.

- Drag the scroll box up or down (in the vertical scroll bar) or left or right (in the horizontal scroll bar) to move up, down, left, or right in the document.

- Click the dark gray area above, below, to the left, or to the right of the scroll box to move up, down, left, or right in the document by one window length or width.

You also can move around a Word for Windows document by using the following key combinations:

Key Combination	Effect
←	Moves the insertion point one character to the left.
→	Moves the insertion point one character to the right.
↑	Moves the insertion point up one line.

Key Combination	Effect
↓	Moves the insertion point down one line.
Ctrl+←	Moves the insertion point one word to the left.
Ctrl+→	Moves the insertion point one word to the right.
Home	Moves the insertion point to the beginning of the line.
End	Moves the insertion point to the end of the line.
PgUp	Moves the insertion point up one page.
PgDn	Moves the insertion point down one page.
Ctrl+Home	Moves the insertion point to the beginning of the document.
Ctrl+End	Moves the insertion point to the end of the document.

Task Reference

The Task Reference is an alphabetical listing of Word for Windows features and commands. To learn the basics of creating multiple columns in your documents, for example, see *Columns*. If you want to learn how to set up a bulleted list, see *Bullets*.

Adding Text

You may find that you need to change a document by adding or replacing text after the document is complete. By the same token, any time you open up a document to continue work on it, you're adding text to it. In Word for Windows, you can add text to existing text with some simple editing features.

To add text to any document, you can either type in new text or cut and paste text from another document, or even merge another text file with the current one (it's called Inserting a file). Normally, Word functions in what's called *Insert mode*, where typed text is added to the document without overwriting anything else. Otherwise, you're in *Overtype mode*, which overwrites existing text with the new text you're typing.

If you're in Overtype mode, the status bar provides an OVR indicator at the bottom of the Word window, which does not appear if you're in Insert mode.

To insert text

Insert mode (the default mode) inserts new text at the insertion point. Existing text moves forward to make room for the new text.

1 Position the insertion point where you want to insert new text.

2 Type the new text. Existing text moves to the right and wraps to the next line.

To type over existing text

Overtype mode replaces existing text with the new text. As with inserting text, much depends on whether you're in Insert or Overtype mode. The INS or Insert key is used to toggle between the two modes, and the OVR indicator in the status bar shows whether you're in Overtype mode.

1 Position the insertion point where you want to begin typing over existing text.

2 Press Ins (the Insert key) to turn on Overtype mode.

The OVR indicator appears in the status bar.

3 Type the new text over the old text.

4 Press Ins again to return to Insert mode.

Also see the *Insert File*, *Cut*, *Copy*, and *Paste* sections in this book.

Alignment

Text alignment is the process of aligning text relative to the left and right margins and the center of the page. For example, text aligned to the left side of the page or column results in a "ragged right" appearance, which is warm and readable. Most conventional and office correspondence is done with a ragged right, left side alignment.

Justified text aligns the words to both the left and right margins. It's used in multiple-column newsletters, newspapers, magazines, and other documents that need an orderly look.

To align text

1 Select the text you want to align (you can select the entire document with the Edit Select All command).

or

Place the insertion point at the beginning of your new document or where you want to enter new text.

2 Choose the Format Paragraph command.

The Paragraph dialog box appears.

3 Select one of the following Alignment options at the bottom right corner:

Option	Effect
Left	Aligns text flush with the left margin (the default).
Centered	Centers text between the left and right margins.
Right	Aligns text flush with the right margin.
Justified	Spreads text between the left and right margins by expanding or contracting the space between words.

Shortcut

You can also align text by clicking the Alignment buttons on the Formatting toolbar.

See also *Format Paragraph* and *Toolbar*.

Annotations

You can insert comments and reminders, called *annotations*, into a document. Annotations are handy when you want to add comments and notes to a document, but don't want them to interrupt the flow of your main text. *Annotation marks* identify each annotation with your initials and a number.

Word for Windows hides annotations unless you display them or convert them to text. You can print the annotations with the document or you can print just the annotations.

To insert an annotation

1 Position the insertion point where you want to insert the annotation.

2 Choose the Insert Annotation command.

The Annotation pane will appear at the bottom of the document window. Word for Windows inserts your initials (from the Tools Options User Info dialog box) and numbers the annotation (in the order that you create it).

3 Type the text of the annotation in the Annotation pane. You can enter up to 50 lines of text. You can use bold, underline, italic, or any text format.

4 Choose the Close button to return to the document.

See also *User Information*.

To display or hide annotation marks

1 Choose the Tools Options command.

The Options dialog box appears.

2 Choose the View tab.

3 To display annotation marks where you inserted annotations, select the Hidden Text check box (from the Nonprinting Characters options).

To hide annotation marks, deselect the Hidden Text check box.

4 Choose OK or press Enter to return to the document.

To view annotations

1 Select the annotation mark for the annotation you want to view.

2 Choose the View Annotations command.

or

Double-click on the Annotation mark if they can be viewed in your document.

The Annotation pane appears, occupying part of the screen below your document.

3 After reading the annotation, choose the Close button to close the Annotation pane and return to the document.

or

Press F6 to keep the Annotation pane open and return to the document.

To convert an annotation to text

1 Select the annotation mark for the annotation you want to convert to text.

2 Choose the View Annotations command.

The Annotation pane appears.

3 Select the text of the annotation inside the annotation pane. Do not include the annotation mark or the paragraph mark at the end of the annotation.

4 Choose the Edit Cut command or press Ctrl+X.

5 Position the insertion point in the document where you want to insert the text of the annotation.

6 Choose the Edit Paste command or press Ctrl+V.

The annotation now appears in the document as normal text.

7 Select the annotation mark for the annotation you converted.

8 Press Del to delete the annotation and its mark.

9 Choose the Close button to close the Annotation pane and return to the document.

To print the document and annotations

1 Choose the File Print command or press Ctrl+P.

The Print dialog box appears.

2 Choose the Options button.

The Options dialog box appears, automatically displaying the Print Options folder.

3 From the Include with Document options, select the Annotations check box.

4 Choose any other printing options (see *Print*).

5 Choose OK or press Enter to close the Options dialog box.

6 Choose OK or press Enter to print the document and annotations.

The annotations print on a separate page at the end of the document text.

See also *Print*.

To print only the annotations

1 Choose the File Print command or press Ctrl+P.

The Print dialog box appears.

2 From the Print What box, select Annotations.

3 Choose OK or press Enter to print the annotations.

AutoCorrect

With this feature, you can save tedious spell-checking and retyping through automatic correction of minor spelling errors. Frequently, you may find yourself entering **teh** instead of **the**, or **adn** instead of **and**. AutoCorrect allows you to fix these automatically without bothering to type them over. You can add your own AutoCorrect entries, and use the feature to replace abbreviations with longer and harder-to-type entries (such as "asap" with "as soon as possible").

To enable and use AutoCorrect

1 Choose the Tools AutoCorrect command.

   The AutoCorrect dialog box appears.

2 The following AutoCorrect checkbox options are offered:

Option	Effect
Change Straight Quotes to Smart Quotes	Automatically changes the default neutral quotes to "Smart Quotes."
Correct TWo INitial Capitals	Automatically repairs accidentally doubled capital letters at the beginning of a word.
Capitalize First Letters in Sentences	Automatically capitalizes the first letters in sentences if the typist misses them.
Capitalize Names of Days	Capitalizes the first letter of Monday, Tuesday, and so on, if necessary.
Replace Text as You Type	If this checkbox is enabled, AutoCorrect will replace mistakes in text as you type, and the following AutoCorrect options are enabled:
Replace	Type the misspelled word you wish to replace in this Text entry box.

continues

Option	Effect
With	In this text entry box, type in the corrected text for replacement.
	Just below the **R**eplace and **W**ith text boxes, the AutoCorrect entry list is displayed, showing all the Replace and With entries currently available.

3 To add the new AutoCorrect entry to the list, choose the **A**dd button. The new AutoCorrect entry will be added.

4 When you're finished with your AutoCorrect entries and have selected the options you want enabled, choose OK or press Enter.

To use a glossary entry

1 Position the insertion point where you want to insert the glossary entry.

2 Type the name of the glossary entry.

3 Press F3 to insert the glossary entry.

AutoFormat

AutoFormat provides a fast and powerful shortcut for those who need to format a document, but don't have time to create a large selection of styles and apply them to each paragraph. AutoFormat, based on the type of document, combines the template for the document with a selection of styles provided by Word to create a specially formatted document. Headings, paragraphs, lists, and other document elements can automatically be formatted.

To auto format a full document

1 Choose the Format AutoFormat command.

The AutoFormat dialog box appears.

2 To format all the text in a document, choose OK or press Enter.

3 When the autoformatting finishes, the AutoFormat dialog reappears, listing three options: To Accept or Reject All changes, to Review Changes, and to Choose a custom look with Style Gallery. An AutoFormat Options button is also offered, which is described later in this section.

4 Choose the Accept button to accept all formatting changes or choose the Reject All button to reject all formatting changes.

If you want to review each formatting change, use the steps in the following section.

To review each formatting change

1 Choose the Review Changes button.

The Review AutoFormat Changes dialog box appears. The Description pane should read No revisions selected. Use Find buttons or select a revision.

2 To begin reviewing individual format changes, choose the Find button showing the right arrow (which moves you forward through the document). The Reject button will be enabled.

3 If the change is not acceptable, choose the Reject button.

4 To review a previous change in the document, choose the Find button showing the left arrow.

To change AutoFormat options

1 Choose the Format AutoFormat command.

The AutoFormat dialog box appears.

2 Select the Options button.

The Options dialog box appears, with the AutoFormat folder displayed.

3 Select any options by clicking on the appropriate checkboxes.

4 Choose OK or press Enter.

AutoText (formerly Glossary)

AutoText, formerly the Glossary command, inserts text, graphics, and other objects into your documents from a global "glossary," which is essentially a holding place for objects (such as pictures, tables, paragraphs of text, and so on) which you may want to use in any or all of your documents. As you place objects into the AutoText glossary, you assign names to each entry, and AutoText builds up a list of all your entries, which can be used in any of your files. Text can be inserted from the AutoText glossary as either plain text or as formatted text (text retaining its original formatting from Microsoft Word).

To create an AutoText entry

1 Select the text, table, graphic, or other object you want to store as an entry. The amount of information you can store depends on the amount of available memory.

2 Choose the Edit AutoText command.

The AutoText dialog box appears.

3 Type a name (up to 31 characters, including spaces) for the glossary entry in the Name text box.

> ### Tip
> Keep your names for AutoText entries as clear as possible, and as short as possible.

4 If your AutoText entry is text, select from the following Insert As options:

Option	Effect
Insert As Formatted Text	Inserts the AutoText glossary entry as plain, unformatted text.
Plain Text	Retains the original Word 6 text formatting in the AutoText glossary entry.
Preview	The preview window shows the AutoText entry as it will appear in your document.

5 Choose the Add button to store the data as an AutoText glossary entry.

6 To delete an AutoText entry on the list, select it in the Name list and choose the Delete button.

7 Select the OK button or press Enter to return to the document.

To add an AutoText entry to the document

1 Place the insertion point in the location of the document where you want to place the AutoText entry.

2 Type in the name of the AutoText entry and press the F3 key.

The AutoText glossary entry will be inserted.

or

2 Choose the Edit AutoText command.

The AutoText dialog box appears.

3 From the Name list, select the AutoText entry you wish to insert into your document.

4 Choose the Insert button.

The AutoText dialog box will disappear, and the entry will be inserted into your document.

To store text from different locations in a document, or from several documents as a single glossary entry, and to recall that glossary entry into a document, you can use the Spike.

See also *Spike* and *Template*.

Bold

Bolding type is done to add emphasis to text, or to draw attention to headings. Bolding type is one of the most common operations you'll perform in Microsoft Word.

To add boldfacing to text

1 Select the text you want to be bold.

2 Choose the Format Font command.

> **Shortcut**
>
> Choose the boldface button on the Formatting toolbar. You can also press Ctrl+B to bold selected text.

3 Under Font Style, select Bold.

Bookmarks

The bookmark option enables you to mark selected text with an invisible bookmark, which is a powerful tool for numerous operations. It can be used to mark selected text, graphics, rows or columns within a table, to mark the current location of the insertion point, and other things. When you apply a bookmark, square brackets ([]) appear at the start and end of the item you select. You can use a bookmark so that the place that is marked is easily found for future work or later revisions.

Bookmarks can also be used to help create cross-references to any marked items (in fact, it's a good idea to use bookmarks as your organizing tool for cross-referencing in your document. See the Cross-Referencing section for more details). Page ranges can also be marked for an index entry (see *Indexes*).

To insert a bookmark

1 Move the insertion point to the location you want to mark or select the text, graphic or other item you want to mark.

> **Tip**
>
> You can insert up to 450 bookmarks in one document.

2 Choose the **Edit B**ookmark command or press Ctrl+Shift+F5.

The Bookmark dialog box appears.

3 Type the name of the bookmark in the **B**ookmark Name text box. A bookmark name can have 1 to 20 characters; can contain letters, numbers, and the underscore (_) character, but not spaces; and must begin with a letter.

4 Choose OK or press Enter to insert the bookmark.

To find a bookmark

1 Choose the **Edit G**o To command or press F5.

The Go To dialog box appears.

2 Select Bookmark from the Go to **W**hat list box.

3 Type the bookmark name in the **E**nter Bookmark Name text box, or choose a bookmark name in the pop-up list.

4 Choose Go To or press Enter to find the bookmark.

Borders

Word's Borders and Shading feature draws lines and
boxes to enclose paragraphs, graphics, or table cells.
You can simply select any of those elements to place a
border around them, or use a frame to enclose the item
and then define the borders and shading of the frame in
the same way. Borders are often used to lend emphasis
or visual impact to a document item, or to help lend
structure to documents such as newsletters and other
multi-column layouts. Borders appear both on-screen
and printed.

To add a border

1 Select the paragraph, graphic, or table cells you
   want to enclose with a border.

2 Choose the Format Borders & Shading command.

   The Paragraph Borders & Shading dialog box
   appears, with the Borders folder displayed.

3 From the Preset options, select Box.

   A shadowed border can also be used.

4 From the Line options, select a line style.

5 Choose OK or press Enter to add the border.

For information about frames and borders, see *Frames*.

To remove a border

1 Select the paragraph, graphic, or table cells from
   which you want to remove a border.

2 Choose the Format Borders & Shading command.

   The Paragraph Borders & Shading dialog box
   appears, with the Borders folder displayed.

3 From the three Preset thumbnail border types,
   select None.

4 Choose OK or press Enter to remove the border.

To add a line

1 Select the paragraph, graphic, or table cells to which you want to add a line.

2 Choose the Format Borders & Shading command.

 The Paragraph Borders & Shading dialog box appears, with the Borders folder displayed.

3 From the Preset options, select None.

4 Click on the Border sample where you want to insert the line.

 Black arrows in the Border sample indicate where the line will appear in the document.

5 From the Line options, select a line style.

6 Choose OK or press Enter to add the line.

Tip

You also can create a frame around text and graphics (see *Graphics*).

Borders & Shading

The Format Borders & Shading command enables you to place borders and boxes around text, tables, and illustrations for visual emphasis, and to add a desktop-published effect to documents. For example, a border is often placed around chapter headings to draw attention to them, or to set them apart from the text. Special paragraphs that convey important information in a book often have borders defined for them as well.

Borders can be shadowed, and in various Windows default colors, as well as shaded in various patterns. Borders can also have lines or "edges" removed.

To apply a border

1 Choose the text, illustration, label, or other object around which you want to place a border.

2 Choose the Format Borders & Shading command.

The Paragraph Borders & Shading dialog box appears.

3 Select either of the two different borders: Box or Shadow.

The Border display shows the border lines or shadows currently used for the selection. Black arrowheads indicate a border line or edge. Border lines can be added in the same way to a vacant area. Clicking the mouse on any border line deletes it.

4 Set border options from the following choices:

Option	Effect
From Text	Specifies the border distance from the selected text in points.
Color	Specifies the color of the border or shadow box.
Style	Offers varying widths and styles of lines for the border.

To add shadowing and shading to a border

1 Choose the text, illustration, label, or other object you want to format.

2 Choose the Format Borders & Shading command.

The Paragraph Borders & Shading dialog box appears.

To use a shadowed border:

3 In the Borders folder, select the Shadow preset.

A shadowed box appears in the Border display.

> **Tip**
>
> Text, illustrations, and other objects can have borders and shadowed boxes placed around them. Frames can be used, but are not required. The key difference between a border and a frame is that frames are free-standing: text can flow around them, and they can be moved anywhere and resized at will; borders are attached only to the object they're assigned to, and don't have the flexibility that frames do.

4 Choose a Line Style, if necessary. (If the default line style is not desirable, any line style from the list can be selected.)

5 Choose the Shading tab, and then choose from the following Shading options:

Shading Fill Option	Effect
Shading	Specifies the visual pattern or color depth for the shading.
Foreground	Specifies the shading foreground color.
Background	Specifies the shading background color.

> **Tip**
>
> Thinner shadows tend to look better on the page.

6 Choose OK or press Enter.

See *Frames* for more information on that topic.

Bullets

Bullets set off sections of text by using symbols such as dots or diamonds for each item in a list or paragraph. Bulleted lists used emphasize each point in the list. You can create bullets in Word for Windows, or select from a number of bullet types. Any character in your fonts can also be used as a bullet. Be creative!

To add bullets

1 Select the text to which you want to add bullets.

2 Choose the Format Bullets and Numbering command.

   The Bullets and Numbering dialog box appears.

3 Choose the Bulleted option tab (it should already be displayed).

   The folder displays six different bulleted list styles.

4 From the Bulleted folder, select a bullet style.

5 Choose OK or press Enter.

To modify bullets in the Format Bullets and Numbering dialog box examples

1 From the Bulleted folder, choose Modify.

   The Modify Bulleted List dialog box appears. Here, colors, bullet positions, alignments, and point size can be changed. You can also enable or disable hanging indents here.

2 Select a different Bullet character from the six thumbnails displayed or select the Bullet button to view other bullet characters available in the current symbol font.

3 The Symbol dialog box appears. The default typeface used is Symbol. Select another font from the Symbols From list box if desired, and then select a bullet character.

4 Choose OK or press Enter.

> ## Tip
>
> The Adobe Zapf Dingbats font has many
> attractive bullet characters which can be
> used to lend a distinctive touch.

5 To turn hanging indents on or off, select the Hanging Indent check box.

6 To change the hanging indent distance, type a different indent value in the Distance from Indent to Text text box, or click the up or down arrows to increase or decrease the distance.

7 To change the width of the space between the bullets in the list and the text, enter a new value in the Distance from Bullet to Text text box, or click the up or down arrows to increase or decrease the value.

8 Choose OK or press Enter to add the bullets.

> ## Tip
>
> To add bullets to items in a list, you also
> can click the Bulleted List button on the
> toolbar.

See also *Lists*.

Captions

Captions provide titles and explanatory information for illustrations and other figures in a document. Word for Windows 6 now offers an enhanced Caption feature. When you add figures, illustrations, tables and other objects to a document, Word can automatically add a basic caption to each, numbered sequentially and with a proper label. Captions can, of course, be added manually, with optional explanatory text added to each caption.

Captions are usually created with a number, and a short sentence of explanatory text.

To add a caption manually

1 Select the illustration, table, or other object to which you wish to add a caption.

2 Choose the Insert Caption command.

The Caption dialog box appears.

3 The Label pop-up list allows you to change the caption to any of the three default options: equations, figure, and table. The caption will read accordingly. Choose one of the label types from the list.

4 Choose OK or press Enter.

The caption appears below the illustration.

To add new captioning labels to the default list

1 Choose the Insert Caption command.

The Caption dialog box appears.

2 Choose the New Label button.

The New Label dialog box appears.

3 In the New Label text box, type in the caption label you want.

4 Choose OK or press Enter.

The new caption label is added to the caption entry list.

To change the caption numbering format

1 Select the caption you want to reformat.

2 Choose the Insert Caption command.

The Caption dialog box appears.

3 Choose the Numbering button.

The Caption Numbering dialog box appears.

4 Choose the numbering you want from the Format pop-up list.

5 To include chapter numbers in the numbering scheme, choose the Include Chapter Number checkbox.

6 To choose a different separator character, such as a hyphen (the default), a period, colon, or other character, select it from the Use Separator pop-up list.

7 Choose OK or press Enter.

To activate Auto Captioning

1 Choose the Insert Caption command.

The Caption dialog box appears.

2 Choose the AutoCaption button.

The AutoCaption dialog box appears.

A list of objects that can be inserted into your documents displays in the Add Caption When Inserting box. You can select any or all of the option checkboxes. When any of the selected object types are placed in the document, captions are automatically added. You can select a label type (Figure, Table, and so on) for each object type, and select the position of the automatically placed caption.

3 Choose the object type or types for which you want to enable caption insertion.

4 Choose OK or press Enter.

Center Text

Centering text is generally done with chapter headers and subheaders, as well as headers and footers of a document. You can center text, graphics, and other objects in the middle of the page or center between left and right margins of a column. Text is centered horizontally on the page.

To center text

1 Select the text you want to place in the center of the page or column, or place the insertion point at the location where centered text is to be entered in the document.

2 Choose the Center Text button on the Formatting toolbar.

Change Case

Word's Change Case feature is used to quickly change the case of a letter, word, sentence, or any quantity of selected text. At times, you'll notice that you accidentally hit the Caps Lock key and type a chunk of text in your document. Instead of erasing the whole thing and starting over, simply use the Change Case feature.

To change the case of selected text

1 Select the text for case changing.

2 Choose the Format Change Case command.

The Change Case dialog box appears.

3 Choose the case changing option button from the five listed: Sentence case, lowercase, UPPERCASE, Title Case, or tOGGLE cASE.

4 Choose OK or press Enter.

> **Tip**
>
> To speed things up, try creating a macro for Change Case using the steps above. For more information, see *Macro*.

Clipboard

The Clipboard is a Windows feature that all Windows applications can use. It stores data temporarily so that you can pass the data from document to document or from application to application, or between different places in the same document.

If you're new to Windows or Word for Windows 6, the Clipboard is a temporary storage place where cut or copied text, graphics, and other information is stored for use elsewhere. The Clipboard is automatically used by Windows applications, and it is also represented as an icon on the Windows desktop so that you can click on it and quickly view its contents.

Clipboard commands

The following Word for Windows commands use the Clipboard:

Command	Effect
Edit Cut Ctrl+X	Cuts selected text or graphics from a document. The data is removed from the document and stored on the Clipboard.
Edit Copy Ctrl+C	Copies selected text or graphics from a document. The data remains in the document, and a copy is stored on the Clipboard.
Edit Paste Ctrl+V	Pastes a copy of the Clipboard's contents into a document at the insertion point.

Shortcut

You can execute the Clipboard by clicking the Cut, Copy, and Paste buttons on the Standard toolbar.

See also *Copy*, *Cut*, *Paste*, and *Toolbar*.

Close

While you're working with Word 6, you'll always be closing and opening files. You'll also be opening and closing dialog boxes even more frequently. Here's how.

To close a document

Choose the **F**ile **C**lose command or press Ctrl+F4. Word for Windows closes the document and clears the screen. If you close a document without saving it, a dialog box asks whether you want to save any changes you made.

Shortcut

Any time you have any kind of window open—an application window, a document window in Word, or a dialog box—you can double-click on the Control menu box at the top left corner of the window to close it.

Sometimes, if you haven't saved a file, you are prompted to do so after you double-click on the Control menu box. Make sure you always save your current work before closing a window.

Remember also that you can have multiple document windows open inside the Word application window.

To close a dialog box

You can use any of the following methods to close a dialog box:

- Double-click the Control menu box (which resembles a file drawer handle) at the left end of the dialog box's title bar.

- Press Alt+space bar to open the Control menu for the dialog box, and then choose Close.

- Press Alt+F4.

- Choose the OK button to save any changes you made and close the dialog box.

- Choose the Cancel button or press Esc to abandon any changes you made and close the dialog box.

- Choose the Close button to close a dialog box that does not contain a Cancel button. When you choose the Close button, however, some dialog boxes save any changes you made.

To close a document window or an application window

Use either of these methods to close a document window or the Word application program:

- Double-click the Control menu box (which resembles a file drawer handle) at the left end of the window's title bar.

- Press Alt+space bar to open the Control menu and then choose Close.

Tip

Note that the Control menu for document windows and the application window is the same.

Columns

Use columns to create parallel columns, newspaper columns, or uneven columns for desktop publishing effects. A single page can have multiple columns in a multi-page document (by using Sections), or an entire document can have multiple columns per page.

Use parallel columns to help build a table. Use newspaper columns to create newsletters, newspapers, and brochures. Text flows from one column to the next until all the text is used.

Uneven columns are two or more columns of varying width on the page, which adds another effect to any page of a newsletter or other document. An uneven column page is often used as the title page of an article or a chapter.

To create parallel columns from existing text

1 Use paragraph marks, commas, or tabs to separate the text you want to convert to parallel columns.

2 Select the text you want to convert to columns.

3 Choose the Table Convert Text To Table command.

The text appears in parallel columns. Gridlines divide the table into columns and rows.

4 To hide the gridlines, choose the Table Gridlines command.

To change the width of parallel columns

1 To change a column's width, click the top border of the column and then choose the Table Column Width command.

2 The Column Width dialog box appears. Type a new width in the Width of Column text box or use the up and down arrows to adjust the value.

> ## Shortcut
>
> To convert selected text to parallel columns, you can also click the Table button on the Standard toolbar.

To create newspaper columns and uneven columns

In newspaper columns, text begins at the top of the column, continues to the bottom of that column, and then continues from the top of the next column. In all column presets, text flows automatically from one column to the next.

Tip

Newspaper columns are a more specialized tool for page layout. You'll need to think about how you want your document to look before you use this feature.

1 Select the text you want to format in newspaper columns, or position the insertion point where you want to begin the columns.

2 Choose the Format Columns command.

The Columns dialog box appears.

3 Type a number in the Number of columns text box or select a predefined column format from the available presets:

One	Single column (default)
Two	Double columns, evenly sized
Three	Triple columns, evenly sized
Left	Two columns, uneven left
Right	Two columns, uneven right

4 Adjust the number of columns from any preset with the Number of Columns text box. The Preview will show how the new column layout will appear.

Tip

Depending on the size of your page, limit the number of columns. On an 8 1/2 by 11-inch page, more than three columns usually do not look good.

5 From the Apply To options, specify whether you want to format the Whole Document or the Selected text. The Preview window adjusts accordingly.

6 Choose OK or press Enter to create the columns.

7 Choose the View Page Layout command to view the newspaper columns.

> ## Shortcut
>
> To convert the selected text to newspaper columns, you can also click the Columns button on the Standard toolbar, hold down the left mouse button, and then drag the mouse to highlight the number of columns you want to create.

Compare Versions

The Compare Versions feature compares two versions of a document, and displays the differences. Comparing is often necessary to supervise changes in a document, to ensure that one version of a document is more up-to-date than another, or to check editing changes.

When two versions of the same file are compared, the document currently displayed shows all the revisions relative to the other document in a different color. Text deleted from the more recent version of the document appears in colored strikethrough, and more recently added text appears in colored underlined text.

> ## Caution!
>
> Save a backup copy of the original document with a different file name before you begin making comparisons. You can return the original file if you decide not to keep the changes.

To compare two versions of a document

1 Open the current version of the document you want to compare.

2 Choose the Tools Revisions command.

The Revisions dialog box appears.

3 Choose the Compare Versions button.

The Compare Versions dialog box appears.

4 In the Original File Name text box, type the name of the version (of the same document) you want to compare to the current, or select it from the file list.

5 Choose OK or press Enter.

The edited document appears on-screen. Revision marks indicate added, replaced, deleted, and moved text. For information on accepting or rejecting revisions, see *Revision Marks*.

To remove all revision marks

Choose the Edit Undo Revision command (it may be several Undo levels deep, but it can still be executed).

See also *Revision Marks*.

Compatibility Options

Compatibility options allow the user to ensure that word processing files imported from other applications can be converted and used with the fewest possible problems. Font substitutions can be made to seamlessly compensate for bringing in files that use fonts different from those on your system.

To adjust compatibility options for specific applications programs

1 Choose the Tools Options command.

The Options dialog box appears.

2 Choose the Compatibility tab.

The Compatibility options appear.

3 To adjust the compatibility defaults for any specific application program, select that program from the Recommended Options For entry box.

As each program is selected, the compatibility options list will change to show a different set.

4 A list of checkbox options displays in the Options area. Each word processing program (WordPerfect, Word for DOS, etc.) will have certain checkboxes selected. Any can be selected or disabled.

5 Choose OK or press Enter.

To change font substitution specifications

Sometimes, you'll receive documents from other people's computers which have fonts in them that are not on your computer. In situations like this, you'll have to go through a quick Font Substitution process to fix this problem. You use fonts that are on your system (Printer fonts, TrueType or Adobe Postscript, for example) to substitute for the original ones in the document.

1 Choose the **T**ools **O**ptions command.

The Options dialog box appears.

2 Choose the Compatibility tab.

The Compatibility options appear.

3 Choose the Font **S**ubstitution button.

The Font Substitution dialog box appears. There are two key entry lists: Missing Document Font, and Substituted Font. The Missing Document Font entries reflect the typefaces originally embedded in the current document which are not present in your system.

4 Select the missing document font requiring substitution by clicking on it. The highlight bar will be placed over it and its substitute.

5 Under the **S**ubstituted Font entry box, select the font you want to use as a substitute in the document.

The newly substituted font displays in the current font list above.

6 Choose OK or press Enter.

Convert File

Each word processor program or other application creates its own type of file, called a *format*. Files frequently must be converted to be readable to other programs. For example, you may convert a WordPerfect file to be readable in Microsoft Word. Word's file conversion capabilities enable reading of files to and from other formats so that you can exchange files with other programs. It's done simply: during the opening and saving of files.

To convert a file from another format

1 Choose the File Open command or press Ctrl+O.

2 From the Directories list box, select the directory that contains the file you want to open.

3 Choose the file you want to open by highlighting it.

4 Select the Open button.

> **Tip**
>
> You can also double-click on the file name to open it.

If the file is not in Word for Windows format, the Convert File dialog box appears.

5 Select the format from which you want to convert the file.

6 Choose OK or press Enter to begin the conversion process.

To convert a file to another format

See *Save/Save As*.

Available file formats

You can convert files to and from the following formats:

Ami Pro 3.0

ANSI

ASCII

dBASE II, III, III PLUS, IV

DisplayWrite DCA/RTF

IBM 5520 DCA/RTF

Lotus 1-2-3 (DOS) Release 2.01, 2.11, 3.0

Microsoft Excel 2.0, 3.0

Microsoft Word (DOS) 4.0, 5.0, 5.5

Microsoft Word (Macintosh) 4.0, 5.0

Microsoft Word for Windows 1.0, 1.1, 1.1a, 2.0

Multiplan 3.0, 4.2

Rich Text Format (RTF)

Text (DOS)

WordPerfect 4.1, 4.2, 5.0, 5.1, 6.0

WordPerfect for Windows 5.1, 5.2

WordStar 3.3, 3.45, 4.0. 5.0, 5.5

Works (DOS) 2.0 word processor documents

Works for Windows word processor documents

Earlier versions of Word for Windows file formats are fully compatible with Word for Windows 6.0.

Copy

With the copy command, you place selected text on the Clipboard without removing it from the document.

You can paste a copy of the Clipboard's contents to another location in the same document, to a different document, or to a document in another Windows program. (See *Clipboard* for more details.)

To copy text, graphics, or other items to the Clipboard

1 Select the text, picture, or other object you want to copy to the Clipboard.

2 Choose the **Edit Copy** command, or press Ctrl+C to copy the text to the Clipboard without removing it from the document.

> **Tip**
>
> Cutting selected objects also moves them to the Clipboard.

To paste data from the Clipboard to a document

1 Position the insertion point in the document where you want to paste the Clipboard data.

2 Choose the **Edit Paste** command or press Ctrl+V to paste a copy of the text into the document.

> **Shortcut**
>
> You also can copy and paste by clicking the Copy and Paste buttons on the Standard toolbar.

> **Tip**
>
> You can paste the Clipboard's contents into a document any number of times until you cut or copy new text. The new text then replaces the preceding contents of the Clipboard.

Caution!

Unfortunately, if you cut or copy more than one item, you will lose the previous item. Use the Spike to preserve multiple cuts or copies (see *Spike* for more details). Also use Undo to rescue multiple cuts.

To copy text without placing it on the Clipboard (Drag and Drop Copy)

1 Select the text you want to copy, but do not want to place on the Clipboard.

2 Position the mouse pointer anywhere over the selected text.

3 Hold down Ctrl and the left mouse button.

The mouse pointer changes to a box that contains an arrow and dotted insertion point.

4 Drag the pointer to the new location.

5 Release the mouse button and Ctrl to copy the text.

See also *Clipboard*, *Cut*, *Paste*, and *Toolbar*.

Cross-Reference

Cross-references are tools to inform the reader about additional information on the current subject elsewhere in the same document or in other documents. A good example of a cross-reference is the "See also *Clipboard*, *Cut*, *Paste*, and *Toolbar*," shown in the preceding section. Word offers powerful cross-referencing features, including automatic updating during the printing of a document.

To create a cross-reference

1 Type the introductory text for the cross-reference into your document.

2 Choose the Insert Cross-reference command.

The Cross-reference dialog box appears. It is a multitasking dialog box, so you can edit text while the dialog box is on the screen.

3 Select the item type to which the cross-reference will refer, in the Reference Type box. The Cross-reference dialog box will remain visible. (It can also be dragged for a better view of the screen text.)

The Reference Type box lists several types of cross-references, corresponding to the various elements you can have in your document:

Heading

Bookmark

Footnote

Endnote

Equation

Figure

Table

Each type, when selected, also affects the options to be selected in the Insert Reference To box.

4 Inside the Insert Reference To box, select the information type about the referred-to item which you want inserted into the cross-reference. For example, if the Reference Type is a Footnote, select Footnote Number or Page Number.

5 The For Which Footnote box will show a list of the items inside the document: the footnotes, or the headings, and so on. Select the specific item to which you want the cross-reference to refer.

6 After you specify the specific item, choose Insert. The Cross-reference dialog box remains open. To close it, press Enter or choose Cancel.

7 You can create more cross-references by repeating steps 3 through 6.

To create a cross-reference to another document

> ## Caution!
>
> You can create cross-references to other
> documents only if the current document
> and the document to which you want to
> cross-reference are both part of a master
> document.

1 When you're in the master document, choose the
View Master Document command.

2 Put the text insertion point outside of a
subdocument.

3 Choose the Insert Cross-reference command.

4 Select the item type to which the cross-reference
will refer in the Reference Type box.

The Reference Type box lists several types of cross-
references. Each type also affects the options to be
selected in the Insert Reference To box.

5 Inside the Insert Reference To box, select the information type about the referred-to item that you
want inserted into the cross-reference. For example,
if the Reference Type is a footnote, select Footnote
Number or Page Number from the list.

6 The For Which Footnote box shows a list of the
items inside the document: the footnotes, or the
headings, and so on. Select the specific item to
which you want the cross-reference to refer.

7 After the specific item is specified, choose Insert.
The Cross-reference dialog box will remain open.

8 To create more cross-references, repeat steps 2
through 7 until you're done. You can leave the
Cross-reference dialog box while you perform the
process. To close it, press Enter or choose Cancel.

To update all cross-references in a document

1 Choose the Edit Select All command.

2 Press the F9 key.

> ### Tip
> Cross-references update automatically
> when a document is printed.

Customize Toolbar

Customizing toolbars is essentially a drag-and-drop
process. You can do it whenever you don't like the
arrangement of buttons on a toolbar, or when you want
to consolidate several toolbars into one. Word for
Windows 6 features a powerful and handy toolbar
customization feature, in which every function of the
program can be placed on a toolbar.

To customize a toolbar

To ease the process of customizing toolbars, have at
least one or two displayed on the WinWord screen.
Then follow these steps:

1 Choose the Tools Customize command.

2 Choose the Toolbars tab.

3 In the Categories list, select the menu name containing the program functions to include in a toolbar,
such as File, Edit, and so on.

A group of buttons displays in the Buttons box.

To see which function the button activates, read the
Description box when you choose a button.

4 Click and hold any button in the Button box and
drag it to any displayed toolbar.

A new button appears in the toolbar.

5 To remove any button from a toolbar, simply drag the button off the toolbar to the Customize tab.

6 To maintain your changes to toolbars, you can Save Changes In the current file or in Normal.Dot, which enables use of the new toolbars in all documents.

Cut

With the Word 6 cut command, you can cut text, tables, graphics, and other items from a document, storing it on the Clipboard. Then you can paste the cut text to another location in the same document, to a different document, or to a document in another Windows program.

Reminder

Cut removes the selected item from the current document. To restore it, use the Undo command.

To cut text, graphics, tables and other items from a document

1 Select the item or items you want to cut.

2 Choose the Edit Cut command or press Ctrl+X to cut the text from the document and store it on the Clipboard.

Shortcut

You can cut and paste by clicking the Cut and Paste buttons on the toolbar.

Tip

You can paste the Clipboard's contents into a document any number of times until you cut or copy new text. The new text then replaces the preceding contents of the Clipboard.

See *Copy*.

**To move text without storing it on the Clipboard
(Drag and Drop)**

Drag and Drop is the process of selecting any item in
your document and dragging it to where you want it in
your current document, or to another document in the
same application program.

1 Select the text that you want to move, but that you
do not want to store on the Clipboard.

2 Position the mouse pointer anywhere in the selected
text.

3 Hold down the left mouse button.

The pointer changes into a box that contains an
arrow and dotted insertion point.

4 Drag the mouse pointer to the new location.

5 Release the mouse button to move the text to the
new location.

See also *Clipboard, Copy, Paste,* and *Toolbar.*

Date and Time

Word's Date and Time feature inserts the date or time
into a document automatically. The date and time is
received from the computer system.

> ## Reminder
>
> Because Word for Windows uses the
> computer's clock to insert the current date
> and time, you must set the computer's clock
> to the correct date and time.

To insert the date or time

1 Position the insertion point in the document where
you want the date or time to appear.

2 Choose the Insert Date and Time command.

The Date and Time dialog box appears.

3 From the Available Formats list box, select the date and time formats you want Word for Windows to use.

4 Choose OK or press Enter.

Word for Windows automatically inserts the date and time when you print the document.

> ## Shortcut
>
> To insert the date, you can also press Alt+Shift+D. The date format appears as numbers separated by slashes (/). In American standard format, a date such as July 04, 1994 will appear as 07/04/94.

> ## Shortcut
>
> To insert the time, you can also press Alt+Shift+T. The time format appears as hours and minutes separated by a colon (:). In American Standard time, it will appear as HH:MM:SS, or 10:30:25.

Deleting

The deletion process is simple. You can delete a character, a word, a line or lines, a sentence, a paragraph, a block of text, or an entire document.

> ## Reminder
>
> Before you make major changes to a document, use the File Save As command to save a copy of the document with a different name.

> **Caution!**
>
> Del and Backspace are repeating keys.
> If you hold down Del or Backspace rather
> than pressing and releasing the key, Word
> for Windows deletes multiple characters
> and the text to the right of the deleted
> character(s) moves to the left. Use the Undo
> command if your deletion isn't right.

To delete a character

Position the insertion point to the left of the character
you want to delete and then press Del.

or

Position the insertion point to the right of the character
you want to delete and then press Backspace.

To delete a word

Double-click the word you want to delete and then press
Del or the Delete key.

or

Position the insertion point to the right of the word you
want to delete and then press Ctrl+Backspace.

To delete a line or lines

1 Position the mouse pointer in the left margin next to
   the first line of text or the first blank line you want
   to delete.

   The mouse pointer changes to an arrow pointing up
   and to the right.

2 Click the left mouse button to select the line of text
   or blank line.

   or

   Drag the mouse pointer down the left margin to
   select the lines of text or blank lines.

3 Press the Del or Delete key.

To delete a sentence

1 Hold down Ctrl.

2 Position the mouse pointer anywhere over the sentence you want to delete.

3 Click the left mouse button to select the sentence.

4 Press the Del or Delete key.

To delete a paragraph

1 Position the mouse pointer in the left margin next to the paragraph you want to delete.

2 Double-click the left mouse button to select the paragraph.

3 Press the Del or Delete key.

To delete a block of text

Select the text you want to delete and then press Del.

To delete an entire document

1 Position the mouse pointer in the left margin.

2 Hold down Ctrl.

3 Click the left mouse button to select the entire document.

4 Press the Del or Delete key.

Document Summary

Word's Document Summary command describes key information about a document.

A summary consists of a title, a subject (a brief summary of the document), the author's name, and key words for which to search. Each piece of information can have up to 255 characters. Files are sorted according to pieces of information in the document summary.

The document summary includes document statistics, such as the number of times you save a document, total editing time, and whether the document is based on a template.

To create document summary information

1 Choose the File Summary Info command.

The Summary Info dialog box appears.

2 Type the information you want to include in the document summary into the following text boxes:

Text Box	Information
Title	The name of the document.
Subject	A description of the document.
Author	The name of the person assigned to the Word for Windows program during setup or the name of the person who wrote the document.
Keywords	Words for which you may want to search (words that set this document apart from other documents).
Comments	Remarks you want to store with the document for future reference.

Tip

It isn't necessary to place every piece of information in Summary Info—just what you need.

3 Choose OK or press Enter to save the information.

To view document statistics

1   Choose the File Summary Info command.

The Summary Info dialog box appears.

2   Choose the Statistics button.

The Document Statistics dialog box appears.

3   View the information about the document.

4   If you have made changes to the document since you last saved it, choose the Update button to update the statistics.

5   Choose OK or Close to save the statistics.

6   Choose OK again or press Enter to close the Summary Info dialog box.

To print summary information and statistics

1   Choose the File Print command.

The Print dialog box appears.

2   Choose the Options button.

The Options dialog box appears.

3   From the Include with Document options, select the Summary Info check box.

4   Choose OK or press Enter to return to the Print dialog box.

5   Choose OK or press Enter again to print the summary information.

The summary information prints on a separate page at the end of the document.

Shortcut

To have a fast look at document statistics, choose the Insert Document Statistics command.

Drag and Drop

See *Cut*.

Drag and Drop Copy

See *Copy*.

Drawing

Microsoft Word's drawing features allow you to create simple illustrations without leaving the application. Simple flowcharts, small geometric pictures requiring simple spot color, and logos can be drawn for figures in your document. You can use up to 40 preset colors for color fills or line colors.

To create a drawing

Whenever you draw a shape, such as a circle, square, or line, it's considered an Object. You can have many objects in a drawing, and they can be layered behind each other.

1 Choose the View Page Layout command. You can only draw objects on a Word document in Page Layout mode.

2 Choose View Toolbars command.

3 Choose this drawing toolbar from the Toolbars scrolling list.

4 Choose OK or press Enter.

5 Choose any object drawing button in the Drawing toolbar, including Line, Curve, Rectangle, Ellipse, Freeform Polygon, or Caption.

6 Draw the object on the document.

With the drawing object selected, the Color Fill and Line Color buttons, among others, can be selected and the characteristics of the drawn object can be changed.

For more information...

A full discussion of the drawing capabilities in Word for Windows 6 is beyond the scope of this book. For more information on WinWord's drawing features, choose the Help Contents command, or choose the button and press the F1 key.

Drop Caps

A classic typographic effect to draw attention to the beginning of a chapter. Drop Caps are a single large letter at the beginning of the first paragraph of a chapter or other segment of text, enlarged and dropped alongside the first several lines of text. The text flows around the dropped capital letter as if it were an illustration.

1 Select the character at the beginning of the chapter, paragraph, or other document section.

2 Choose the Format Drop Cap command.

The Drop Cap dialog box appears.

3 Choose from the following drop cap options:

Option	Effect
None	Default. No drop cap.
Dropped	Creates a drop cap of the specified size into the current paragraph.
In Margin	Places a drop cap in the margin, showing as a hanging indent.

The font of the dropped capital letter can be changed, as can the number of lines of text it is dropped by, and its distance from the document text.

Tip

Use a different font from the regular text to draw more attention to the drop cap, and thus to the beginning of the chapter.

---

4 Select OK or press Enter.

Endnotes

Like footnotes, endnotes provide references and attributions, and both are produced in much the same way. Endnotes, however, provide references and attributions at the end of a chapter, section, or document. Endnotes are used, for example, to provide a list of sources. They're normally used with lowercase Roman numerals (i, ii, iii). Reference marks in body text indicate a reference to an endnote.

To create an endnote

1 Position the insertion point where you want to place the reference mark.

2 Choose the Insert Footnote command.

The Endnotes and Footnotes dialog box appears.

3 Select the Endnote option.

Note that the option reads `End of document`. Note also that the AutoNumber option changes to lowercase Roman numerals.

4 Choose OK or press Enter.

If you're in Normal view, a window for typing in the endnote text displays at the bottom of the Word screen. If you're in Page Layout view, you can enter the endnote text directly in the document.

Shortcut

To quickly enter an endnote, press
Ctrl+Alt+E.

---

5 Type the endnote text.

6 If you're working in the Normal View, choose the
Close button at the top of the pane.

or

If you're working in Page Layout View, simply scroll
back up the document or use the Go To command.

Tip

You can move endnotes by selecting the
reference mark and dragging it to another
place in the document. Word automatically
updates the reference numbers for you if
the endnote references are numbered
automatically.

**To customize numbering in the Footnotes and
Endnotes dialog box**

1 Choose the Tools Options command.

The Note Options dialog box appears, with the All
Endnotes folder displayed. You can make the
following changes:

Option	Description
Place At	Endnotes can be set up for placement at the end of a section or the end of a document with this entry list.
Number Format	Endnote numbering formats can be changed with this entry list. Numbering formats

Option	Description
	include numerals, upper- and lowercase Roman numerals, upper- and lowercase letters, and text symbols.
Start At	Set the starting endnote number or letter with the Start At text box. Use the up and down arrows on the box to raise or lower the value.

2 Choose OK or press Enter.

Envelopes

Word offers a quick and handy feature to print addresses on envelopes. Addresses can be printed on different sizes of envelopes. Envelopes can be printed immediately, or an envelope can be included in a document. You can also specify a return address.

To print an address on an envelope

An envelope can be printed from any document.

1 Place the insertion point at the beginning of the mailing address text in your document.

2 Choose the Tools Envelopes and Labels command.

The Envelopes and Labels dialog box appears. The mailing address appears in the **D**elivery Address text box. You can enter a new address if necessary, or edit the current one.

Shortcut

You can also access the Envelopes and
Labels dialog box by clicking the Envelope
button on the Word for Windows 2.0
toolbar.

3 To include a return address, type that address in
the **R**eturn Address box. If you do not want to print
a return address on the envelope, select the Omit
check box.

4 Choose the **O**ptions button.

5 From the Envelope **S**ize options, select the size of
the envelope.

6 Choose OK or press Enter.

7 Select the **P**rint button to print the envelope.

Tip

If you want an address different from the
first in the letter that appears in the Delivery Address box, select the address text
you want in the envelope, and then choose
the Tools Envelopes and Labels command.
The address appears in the Delivery
Address box.

To set a default return address on an envelope

1 Choose the **T**ools **O**ptions command.

2 Choose the User Info tab, and the User Info folder
appears.

The User Info dialog options appears.

3 To enter a default return address, type that address
in the **M**ailing Address box.

4 Choose the OK button.

Equation Editor

The Equation Editor enables you to create scientific and mathematical equations in the Equation Editor window. You can then insert the equations into documents as objects. The Equation Editor is an add-in program you can use with Word for Windows and other Microsoft programs.

To create an equation

1 Position the insertion point where you want the equation to appear in your document.

2 Choose the Insert Object command.

The Object dialog box appears.

3 From the Object Type list, choose Microsoft Equation 2.0 by double-clicking it.

The Equation Editor window appears.

4 Type the equation in the Equation Editor window. You can click special symbols and keywords on the Equation palette to include those symbols or keywords in the equation.

5 Choose the File Exit and Return To Document menu command to exit the Equation Editor window.

Tip

Use the File Update command to update the equation in your document while remaining in the Equation Editor. (Pressing the F3 key will have the same effect.)

To edit an equation

1 Select the equation you want to edit by clicking on it with the mouse.

2 Choose the Edit Object Edit command.

The Equation Editor window appears, displaying the selected equation for editing.

> **Tip**
>
> If you frequently use equations, you can save time by adding the Equation button to the toolbar (see *Toolbar*).

Please note that the Equation Editor is a substantial application, and a description of the functions of the program is beyond the scope of this book. For more information, please see *Using Word Version 6 for Windows,* Special Edition.

Exit

Word's Exit feature, as with many other Windows applications, allows you to exit the application and return to Windows.

To exit Word for Windows and return to Windows

1 Choose the File Exit command or press Alt+F4.

If you did not save your work, a dialog box asks whether you want to save your changes.

2 Choose one of the following buttons:

Option	Effect
Yes	Saves the changes and exits the program.
No	Abandons any changes and exits the program.
Cancel	Cancels the command and remains in the Word for Windows program.

┌─ **Caution!** ─────────────────────

Be careful if you choose No—you will lose
any work you've done since you last saved
the file.

└────────────────────────────────────┘

3 If another dialog box displays the message Do you
want to save the global glossary and command
changes?, choose **Yes** to save the changes or **No** to
abandon the changes.

4 Word will close, and you will be returned to the
Windows Program Manager.

Find and Replace

The Find and Replace option finds and replaces specific
text, character formats, or paragraph formats in a
document. Find and Replace is a powerful word processing option because you can change a word or phrase
scattered throughout an entire document with a simple
procedure instead of performing laborious editing.

Find and Replace can also perform its work on text that
has been formatted in a specific way—text that has been
boldfaced, italicized or underlined, or formatted with a
style. The text to be found can also be specified as a
special character, any of which appears in a document:
em and en dashes, manual page breaks, section breaks,
carets, and so on.

To find and replace text

1 Position the insertion point where you want to begin
the search.

2 Choose the **Edit Find** command.

The Find dialog box appears.

┌─ **Shortcut** ─────────────────────

You can also press Ctrl+F.

└────────────────────────────────────┘

Tip

Even while the Find dialog box is showing,
you can click in the document window and
do basic editing. You can then click back in
the dialog box to make it active again.

---

3 To search for text, type the text you want to find
(up to 255 characters) in the Find What text box.

4 Choose from the following Search options:

Option	Effect
Down, Up, All	Options in the Search entry list that determine the direction for the Find operation.
Match Case	Searches for text with the specified combination of upper- and lowercase letters.
Find Whole Words Only	Searches for whole words only; does not find occurrences of the word that are part of other words.
Use Pattern Matching	Searches for patterns in formatting, such as indented paragraphs and numbered headings.
Sounds Like	Searches for words that sound like the current word to search for.
Search	Specifies the direction of the search. Choose Down to search forward or Up to search backward.

Other buttons under Find include:

Option	Effect
Format	Allows you to search for text according to the following criteria: Font, Paragraph, Language, Style.
Special	Allows searching for numerous special characters and markers that may appear in a document, such as em and en dashes, carets, footnote and endnote markers, and many other typographic signs and entry fields.
Replace	Selecting the Replace button opens up another section of the Find dialog box, in which you can enter the text with which you want to replace the text you Find. (See below for more details.)

For each format choice, you'll see a dialog box under which you select the options for searching.

Tip

In almost any case, using styles as a search criteria is much more effective—assuming you used styles consistently throughout your document!

5 Choose the Find Next button or press Enter.

The search begins, stopping at the first occurrence of the text or format for which you are searching. The Find dialog box remains open.

6 To search for other occurrences of the text or formats, choose the **F**ind Next button or press Enter. If you began the search at the beginning of the document, the message that Word has reached the end of the document appears when the program finds no more occurrences of the text or format. Choose OK or press Enter.

7 Choose the **R**eplace button.

A Replace With text box is inserted below the Find What field.

> **Tip**
>
> Notice that the Format and Special buttons remain available. You can specify any of the same formatting, character, or marker replacements that you would in the Find What text box.

8 In the Replace With text box, type in the replacement text.

Select from the following buttons, depending on the function you want to perform:

Find Next	Finds the next instance of the desired word, phrase, or format.
Replace	Replaces the occurrence of the word.
Replace All	Replaces all instances of the specified word, phrase, or formatting with the replacement in the Replace text box.

> **Shortcut**
>
> You also can continue the search process by closing the Find dialog box and pressing Shift+F4 to find each occurrence of the text or format.

If you began the search in the middle of the document, the message that Word has reached the end of the document appears. `Do you want to continue searching at the beginning?` appears when the program finds no more occurrences of the text or format. Choose **Yes** to search the rest of the document or **No** to stop the search.

9 To stop the search or close the Find dialog box, choose Cancel.

To search for character formats using the Find dialog box

To search for character formats, follow these steps:

1 Choose the Format button, and then choose Font.

The Find Font dialog box appears.

2 Select the character format you want to find, including the font name, the point size, and its character style (Bold, Italic, and so on). See *Font* for more details on the subject of Fonts.

3 Choose OK to return to the Find dialog box, or Cancel if you change your mind.

> **Tip**
>
> The same procedure can be followed to enter replacement information in the Replace With text box (if you chose the Replace button first).

4 To replace text, choose the **R**eplace button.

The Find dialog box changes to the Replace dialog box.

5 Type the text you want to use for replacement (up to 255 characters) in the Re**p**lace With text box.

When the replacement text is entered, press Enter. The search begins. The search text is then entered in the list of text to search for. You can then type in another entry of text. To reuse previous search entries, pull down the list and select them.

6 When the Search text is found, select the Replace button to replace and continue.

7 Replacement text can be set up in the same way as Find text: with paragraph formats, font types, styles, and languages.

8 To automatically replace all search text with replacement text, choose the Replace All button.

9 When you finish, choose Cancel to close the Replace dialog box.

To search for paragraph formats using the Find dialog box

To search for paragraph formats, follow these steps:

1 Choose the Format button and then choose Paragraph.

2 Select the Indents and Spacing and Text Flow specifications you want to find.

3 Choose OK to return to the Find dialog box, or Cancel if you change your mind.

> **Tip**
>
> You can search for and replace styles with other styles in the same manner. The same is also true for text written in foreign languages.

4 To replace text, choose the Replace button.

The Find dialog box changes to the Replace dialog box.

5 Type the text you want to use for replacement (up to 255 characters) in the Replace With text box.

When the replacement text is entered, press Enter. The search begins. The search text is then entered in the list of text to search for. You can then type in another entry of text. To reuse previous search entries, pull down the list and select them.

6 When the Search text is found, select the Replace button to replace and continue.

7 Replacement text can be set up in the same way as Find text: with paragraph formats, font types, styles, and languages.

8 To automatically replace all search text with replacement text, choose the Replace All button.

9 When you finish, choose Cancel to close the Replace dialog box.

Find File

The Find File command enables you to find files on your computer system. Searches can also be saved for future use.

To find files

1 Choose the File Find File command.

The Search dialog box appears, displaying the Saved Searches list and the Search For File Name and Location entry boxes.

2 Select the Search button.

3 Type the name of the file you want to find in the File Name text box.

You can use the asterisk (*) and question mark (?) wildcard characters to find a group of files. To find all files in the current directory, for example, type *.*.

4 To search a different drive, select the drive from the Location list box.

5 To include all subdirectories in a search across an entire drive, select the Include Subdirectories checkbox.

Tip

The Include Subdirectories checkbox is absolutely critical for an effective search, so in almost every case you'll want to make sure this checkbox is enabled!

---

6 Choose the OK button.

After a short time, the Find File dialog box appears, displaying a Listed Files list of all the locations of the searched-for files, and the file contents for each file in the list appear in the Preview Of box on the right side of the Find File dialog box. You can use the mouse to scroll through the document.

7 To open a file, make sure the file is highlighted, and choose the Open button, or double-click it with the mouse.

To select a file or files for Printing, Deleting, Copying, and other commands under the Find File dialog box

1 Select the (first) file name by clicking it.

2 To select additional files that are in sequence, hold down Shift and click the last file name.

To select additional files that are not in sequence, hold down Ctrl and click each file name.

3 Choose the Commands button.

You can choose Open Read Only, Print, Summary, Delete, Copy, or Sorting to execute that command for the selected files.

or

1 In the File Name list box, press ↑ or ↓ to highlight the (first) file you want to select.

2 To select additional files in sequence, press Shift+F8, hold down Shift as you press ↑ or ↓ to highlight the additional file names, and then press Shift+F8 again.

To select additional files that are *not* in sequence, press Shift+F8, press ↑ or ↓ to highlight the next file name you want to select, and then press the space bar. Continue pressing ↑ or ↓ and space bar to select each file, and then press Shift+F8 to complete the selection.

To copy files to another location

1 Find and select the files you want to copy.

2 Choose the Commands button and choose Copy.

The Copy dialog box appears.

3 Type the destination path in the Path text box.

or

Choose the destination drive from the Drives list box and the destination directory from the Directories list box.

4 Choose OK or press Enter to copy the file to a new location.

To delete files

1 Find and select the files you want to delete.

2 Choose the Delete button, or press the Del or Delete key.

The Delete dialog box appears.

3 Choose Yes to delete the files or No to cancel the delete command.

> ## Caution!
> Be careful when deleting files!

The Advanced Search button in the Search dialog box offers the ability to specify searching criteria based on document summary information, and time stamps. You can also search in specific directories only.

The Find File dialog box also offers three different views:

Preview. Displays a visual representation of the currently selected file.

File Info. Displays the File Name, Title, Author, File Size, and Last Saved date of the files on the list.

Summary. Displays more detailed information about the file, including word count, Subject (if any), and other information.

See also *Document Summary*, *Open*, and *Print*.

Font

Word's extensive font handling features allow you to change the typefaces on selected text. A very popular feature of the Windows environment, fonts allow you to add different looks to your text. Fonts can be changed for any amount of selected text, or you can change the default font at the insertion point of the document to any font available.

To change fonts

1 Select the text on which you want to change the font. It can be a single letter, a word, sentence, paragraph, or an entire document. You can select any amount of text in the document.

or

Place the insertion point where you want to change the default typeface, if you want to change the font for text you are about to type.

2 Choose the Format Font command.

The Font dialog box appears.

> **Tip**
>
> The fonts available in the Font list box
> depend on the printer driver you are using,
> your printer's capabilities, and whether you
> installed a print cartridge or a soft font
> package, such as Adobe Type Manager,
> Bitstream FaceLift, or MoreFonts. Formatted
> characters print as they appear on-screen.

3 Choose from the following:

Option	Effect
Font	Specifies the overall look of the character set. A font is also called a *typeface*.
Font Style	Specifies the emphasis of the character. You can select Bold, Italic.
Size	Specifies the character size, in points. The higher the points number, the larger the text will be.
Underline	Specifies None, Single, Double, or Words Only underlining.
Color	Specifies the screen color of a character. You can select from 16 colors.
Strikethrough	Draws a strikethrough line through selected characters.
Superscript	Raises the text above the regular position on the text line. (Typically used for footnotes, or mathematical superscripts.)

continues

Option	Effect
Subscript	Lowers the selected text below the regular position on the text line.
Hidden	Hides characters on the page.
Small caps	Formats text to small capital letters.
All Caps	Formats text for all capital letters.
Preview	Displays the font effects before you apply them.

When text is formatted for any of these options, they will appear on-screen as they do on paper.

4 Choose OK or press Enter.

Keyboard shortcuts

You also can use the following keyboard shortcuts to apply character formats:

> **Tip**
>
> You can change the default font to any font available which is currently selected in the Format Font dialog box. To change the default font for the current document, and new documents in the future, choose the Default button in the Format Font dialog box.

Format	Key Combination
All Caps	Ctrl+Shift+A
Bold	Ctrl+B
Change case	Shift+F3

Format	Key Combination
Double underline	Ctrl+Shift+D
Font	Ctrl+Shift+F
Hidden text	Ctrl+Shift+H
Italic	Ctrl+I
Revert to Default font	Ctrl+Shift+Z
Small Caps	Ctrl+Shift+K
Subscript	Ctrl+=
Format	Key Combination
Superscript	Ctrl+Shift+=
Increase point size	Ctrl+]
Decrease point size	Ctrl+[
Underline	Ctrl+U
Word underline	Ctrl+Shift+W

Tip

To store a collection of character formats and create a particular style to apply to a document, you can use the Style feature (see *Styles*).

Shortcut

You can apply character formats by selecting the **Format Font** command, by using the keyboard shortcuts, or by clicking buttons or selecting formats on the toolbar.

See also *Format Paragraph*, *Toolbar*, and *Styles*.

Footnotes

To refer the reader to a source of information or to provide additional data, you can add footnotes to a document. Footnotes can appear at the bottom of the page, at the end of the text on a page, at the end of a section, or at the end of the document. You can mark footnotes with numbers or a symbol (such as an asterisk).

To create a footnote

1 Position the insertion point where you want to place the reference mark.

2 Choose the Insert Footnote command.

The Endnotes and Footnotes dialog box appears, with the following option buttons for selection:

Option	Effect
Insert Footnote	Specifies that you want to place a footnote in the document.
Endnote	Specifies that you want to place an endnote in the document.
AutoNumber	Specifies the numbering style for the footnotes or endnotes.
Custom Mark	When the button is selected, text box allows you to specify another symbol type.

3 Choose the Footnote button.

Note that the option reads `Bottom of page`. Note also that the AutoNumber option displays numeric characters(1, 2, 3...) as a default.

4 To number footnotes automatically, select the Auto-Numbered Footnote option button.

5 To specify another footnote mark type, choose the Options button. Footnote options available with the Options button include the following:

Option	Effect
Place At	Specifies placing footnotes Beneath Text, or at Bottom of Each Page.
Number Format	Specifies regular numbers, upper- and lowercase Roman numerals, upper- and lowercase letters, and Symbols.
Start At	Specifies where the footnote numbering should start.
Numbering	Selection specifies whether the footnote numbering should be Continuous through the document, Restarted Each Section, or Restarted at Each Page.

6 Choose OK.

If you're in Normal view, a pane for typing in the footnote text displays at the bottom of the Word screen. If you're in Page Layout view, you can enter the footnote text directly in the document.

┌─ **Tip** ─────────────────────────────
│ To view the footnote text on-screen, choose
│ the View Page Layout command (see *View*).
└──────────────────────────────────────

7 Type the footnote text.

8 If you're working in the Normal View, choose the Close button at the top of the pane.

or

If you're working in Page Layout View, simply type in the footnote text.

Format Paragraph

The Format Paragraph option enables you to enhance text and improve the visual appearance of documents. You can change the format of a paragraph by setting tabs, indenting paragraphs, aligning paragraphs, changing line spacing within and between paragraphs, controlling page breaks, and inserting line numbers.

Formatting paragraphs is one of the most important aspects of designing a document. Styles are created largely from paragraph formatting commands (see *Styles* for more information).

To apply paragraph formats

1 Select the paragraph you want to format or place the insertion point where you want to enter new text with specifications.

2 Choose the Format Paragraph command.

The Format Paragraph dialog box appears.

3 Choose the Indents and Spacing tab.

4 Choose from any of the following paragraph format options:

Option	Effect
Indentation	
Left	Indents the paragraph from the left margin.
Right	Indents the paragraph from the right margin.
Special	First Line, Hanging, or None indent types

Option	Effect
By	The distance by which to indent the paragraph.
First Line	Indents the first line from the left indent of the paragraph.
Hanging	Enables a hanging indent.

Tip

You can use positive or negative measurements for the left, centered, and right indents. Positive measurements move the paragraph's edges toward the center of the page. Negative measurements move the paragraph's edges toward the edges of the page. This indent feature is useful for setting hanging indents. An indent of zero moves the paragraph boundaries to the margins.

Spacing

Before	Line spacing above each selected line, in point size.
After	Line spacing below each selected line, in point size.
Line Spacing	Auto specifies the line spacing automatically according to the tallest character on each line. Options for default line spacing include Single, 1.5 lines, Double, At Least (the current point size), Exactly, and Multiple Lines.
	At Least specifies the minimum amount of space between lines (Word for Windows adds additional

continues

Option	Effect
	space as needed). Exactly specifies a fixed amount of space between lines (Word for Windows does not add additional space, even if needed.)
At	Specifies a customized amount of space between lines (in points or lines)
Alignment	
Alignment	Left aligns text at the left margin (the default). Centered centers text between the left and right margins. Right aligns text at the right margin. Justified spreads text evenly between the left and right margins.

To set text flow for paragraph formatting

Text Flow options tell Word how to set paragraphs on the page. For example, options can be set which affect how pages are set up in your document, such as avoiding dangling last lines, or orphans, on a mostly blank page. Setting text flow options ensures an efficient page layout.

1 Select the paragraph you want to format or place the insertion point where you want to enter new text with paragraph formatting specifications.

2 Choose the Format Paragraph command.

The Format Paragraph dialog box appears.

3 Choose the Text Flow tab, and the Text Flow folder appears.

4 Choose from any of the following paragraph format options:

Option	Effect
Pagination	
Widow/Orphan Control	Prevents short words at the end of a paragraph from overlapping.
Keep With **N**ext	Keeps the paragraph and the next paragraph on the same page.
Keep Lines Together	Keeps all the lines of the paragraph on the same page.
Page Break Before	Inserts a page break before the paragraph so that the paragraph appears at the top of the next page.
Line Numbers **S**uppress	Does include line numbers with the Forma**t S**ection Layout command in the line count during pagination.
Don't Hyphenate	Remove hyphenating of page numbers.

The Preview box displays the effect of the paragraph formats you apply.

5 Choose OK to apply the paragraph formats.

Keyboard shortcuts

You also can use the following keyboard shortcuts to apply paragraph formats:

Format	Key Combination
Centered	Ctrl+E
Decrease hanging indent	Ctrl+Shift+T

continues

Format	Key Combination
Decrease indent from left	Ctrl+M
Double spacing	Ctrl+2
Hanging indent	Ctrl+T
Indent from left	Ctrl+N
Justified	Ctrl+J
Left-aligned	Ctrl+L
Normal style	Ctrl+Shift+N
1.5 spacing	Ctrl+5
Remove formatting	Ctrl+Q
Right-aligned	Ctrl+R
Single spacing	Ctrl+1
Style	Ctrl+Shift+S

Tip

To display the effect of paragraph formats on-screen, use the View Page Layout command (see *View*).

Tip

You can apply paragraph formats by selecting the Format Paragraph command, by using the keyboard shortcuts, or by clicking the Indent and Unindent buttons on the Toolbar (see *Toolbar*).

See also *Page Breaks*, *Ruler*, *Styles*, and *Toolbar*.

Frames

Frames are a powerful tool for page layout and document design. You can draw a frame around a block of text, a graphic, or a chart. You can use a frame to change the position of the text or other object on the page. Frames offer greater flexibility than simple borders because they can be used to move page elements, such as blocks of text or pictures, to new positions on the page. Borders and boxes can be added to a frame in the same way as described in the Borders and Shading section.

To create a frame

1 Choose the **View P**age Layout command to switch to Page Layout View.

2 Select the text or other object you want to include in the frame, or place the insertion point where you want a new frame to be located in your document.

3 Choose the **I**nsert **F**rame command or click the Insert Empty Frame button on the Drawing toolbar.

   The frame appears around the selected text, or an empty frame is inserted into the document at the location of the insertion point.

4 Press Enter or click anywhere outside the frame to insert the frame in the document.

> **Shortcut**
>
> To insert a frame quickly, you can click the Frame button on the Word for Windows 2.0 toolbar.

Full Screen View

Full Screen View is a special document view that removes all elements of the Word screen, displaying the document over the entire computer screen. You can still scroll the document and perform edits.

To turn on Full Screen view

1 Choose the View Full Screen command.

   The Word screen elements disappear, leaving the document displayed over the entire screen.

2 To return to the Word screen display, choose the Full button at the bottom right corner of the screen, or press Esc.

Tip

Any screen view (**N**ormal, **P**age Layout, **M**aster Document, or **O**utline) can be used in full screen mode.

Caution!

You can pull down menus with keystrokes by using the Alt key and the appropriate keystroke, but you cannot use the mouse in full screen mode for that purpose. The mouse can still be used to place the insertion point in text, or to select text, for drag and drop, and for other purposes, in full screen mode.

See *View* for more info.

Function Keys

You can execute commands quickly by pressing the following function keys or function key combinations:

Key Combination	Command
F1	Help
Alt+F1	Next field
Alt+Shift+F1	Preceding field

Key Combination	Command
Shift+F1	"What Is" Help
F2	Move text or graphics
Alt+F2	Unassigned
Alt+Shift+F2	File Save
Ctrl+F2	File Print Preview
Shift+F2	Copy text
F3	Edit AutoText
Ctrl+F3	Store in Spike
Ctrl+Shift+F3	Insert Spike and empty contents
Shift+F3	Changes case
F4	Edit Repeat Frame
Alt+F4	File Exit
Ctrl+F4	File Close
Shift+F4	File Find File
F5	Edit Go To
Alt+F5	Preceding application window size
Ctrl+F5	Preceding document window size
Ctrl+Shift+F5	Edit Bookmark
Shift+F5	Preceding position
Key Combination	Command
F6	Next pane
Alt+F6	Next window

continues

Key Combination	Command
Alt+Shift+F6	Preceding window
Ctrl+F6	Next Window
Ctrl+Shift+F6	Preceding window
Shift+F6	Preceding pane
F7	Tools Spelling
Ctrl+F7	Move window
Ctrl+Shift+F7	Update link
Shift+F7	Tools Thesaurus
F8	Extend selection
Ctrl+F8	Size window
Ctrl+Shift+F8	Select column or display or hide tab and paragraph marks
Shift+F8	Shrink selection
F9	Update field
Alt+F9	Reduce application window to icon
Alt+Shift+F9	Go To/Macro button fields
Ctrl+F9	Field characters
Ctrl+Shift+F9	Unlink field
Shift+F9	Switch field codes or results
F10	Menu bar
Alt+F10	Enlarge application window
Ctrl+F10	Enlarge document window

Key Combination	Command
Shift+F10	Cut/Copy/Paste/Font/Paragraph/Bullets and Numbering menu bar
F11	Next field
Ctrl+F11	Lock field
Key Combination	Command
Ctrl+Shift+F11	Unlock field
Shift+F11	Preceding field
F12	File Save **As**
Ctrl+F12	File **O**pen
Ctrl+Shift+F12	File **P**rint
Shift+F12	File **S**ave

Go To

The Go To allows you to quickly move through pages and between objects in a document. Go To allows you to move to any page in the current document, and to move between many different elements of a document, such as bookmarks, sections, endnotes and footnotes, annotations, and other items.

To go to another document page

1 Choose the Edit **G**o To command or press F5.

2 Type the page number you wish to go to.

3 Select the Next button or press Enter.

To go to certain places in Word

1 Choose the **E**dit **G**o To command or press F5.

2 In the Go To What list box, select from the following:

Option	Effect
Page	Go to specified page.
Section	Go to another section of the document.
Line	Go to a specified line of the document.
Bookmark	Go to a specified bookmark.
Annotation	Go to a specified annotation.
Footnote	Go to a specified footnote.
Endnote	Go to a specified endnote.
Field	Go to a field in a form.
Table	Go to a specified table in a document.
Graphic	Go to a specified graphic in a document.
Equation	Go to a specified equation in a document.
Object	Go to a specified object type in a document. The object type can be specified as any OLE object type available to your Windows system.

5 Choose the **Next** button to go to the next page or other selected entity.

6 Choose the **P**revious button to go to the previous page or other selected entity.

Tip

You can move between many items in a document, such as footnotes, endnotes and OLE objects, by numbers. For example, you could indicate +4 or +1 to move four footnotes or one footnote forward, or –3 (3 items back). Select the item type from the list above, then specify the number of items by which you wish to move in the Enter Number text box. Also note that as you select different items in the Go To What list, the Enter Number box caption changes to show the new item chosen (Enter Line Number, Enter Footnote Number, Enter Page Number, and so on).

Grammar

You can use the grammar checker as a proofreading check before you print the document. Grammar checking a document does not eliminate the need for proofreading, but does reduce the amount of proofreading you need to do.

To check grammar in a document

1 Place the insertion point at the place in the document where you wish to begin your grammar check, or anywhere in the current document in which you wish the grammar check to be executed.

2 Choose the **Tools Grammar** command.

The Grammar dialog box appears.

3 If the grammar checker finds an error in grammar or style, choose one of the following options to correct the error or to continue checking grammar:

Option	Effect
Start	Restarts the grammar checker after an editing change.
Ignore	Skips the current suggestion and does not change the sentence.
Change	Executes the suggestion and changes the sentence. If the Change button is unavailable, press Ctrl+Tab or click the document to activate the document, make the changes, and then choose the Start button to continue checking grammar.
Next Sentence	Skips the current suggestion and checks the following sentence.
Ignore Rule	Skips the rule that appears in the Suggestions box (and similar rules within a group of grammar or style rules) for the rest of the document.
Cancel	Exits the grammar checker.
Explain	Provides additional information about the rule.
Undo Last	Undoes the last grammatical change to the document.
Options	Enables you to change the rules.

Errors in grammar are displayed in red in the Grammar dialog box. If the Grammar checker discovers a spelling error, the Spelling dialog box will appear in turn (see *Spelling* for more information).

If you begin checking grammar at the beginning of the document or check a section of the document, Word for Windows displays the Readability Statistics box when it reaches the end of the document or section.

If you begin checking grammar in the middle of the document, Word for Windows displays the message `Do you want to continue checking at the begin-` `ning of the document?` when it reaches the end of the document or section. Choose Yes to continue the grammar checking process at the beginning of the document, or choose No to display the Readability Statistics box.

3 Choose OK when you finish reading the statistics.

Word for Windows returns to the document.

> **Tip**
>
> To ignore spelling errors while checking grammar, choose the Options button in the Grammar dialog box and the Customize Settings button in the Options dialog box. Then choose the Check **S**pelling check box from the Grammar options to deselect the spelling option. If you want to disable the display of the Readability Statistics feature, choose the Options button in the Grammar dialog box and choose the Show **R**eadability Statistics check box to disable it.

See also *Spelling* and *Thesaurus*.

Graphics

Word's graphics handling capabilities enable you to add graphics, or pictures, from a variety of sources such as drawing, charting, or graphing programs to a document.

Word for Windows powerful Microsoft Draw feature enables you to mix text, type, and pictures and to edit and enhance the graphics you create within Microsoft Word.

To create a graphics frame

1 Choose the **View P**age Layout command.

2 Position the insertion point where you want to create the frame.

3 Choose the **I**nsert **F**rame command.

The pointer changes to a cross-hair shape.

4 Use the mouse to position the cross-hair pointer or use the arrow keys where you want the upper left corner of the frame to appear, and then press Enter.

5 Drag the mouse to position the cross-hair pointer where you want the lower right corner of the frame, and then release the mouse button.

or

Use the arrow keys to position the cross-hair pointer where you want the lower right corner of the frame to appear, and then press Enter.

The frame appears in the document. You now can type text in or import a graphic into the frame.

To import a graphic

1 Choose the **View P**age Layout command.

2 Position the insertion point at the top of the frame or at the location where you want to insert the picture in the document.

3 Choose the **I**nsert **P**icture command.

The Picture dialog box appears.

4 From the File **N**ame list box, select the graphic file you want to import. You can import graphics in the following formats into Word for Windows:

Format	File Type
Windows Metafile	WMF
Encapsulated PostScript	EPS

Format	File Type
TIFF	TIF
Computer Graphics Metafile	CGM
HP Graphic Language	HGL
DrawPerfect	WPG
Micrografx Designer 3.0 or Draw Plus	DRW
PC Paintbrush	PCX
Windows Bitmaps	BMP
AutoCAD 2-D	DXF
AutoCAD Plotter	PLT
Lotus 1-2-3 Graphics	PIC

5 To view the graphic before you import it, choose the
Preview Picture button.

6 Choose OK to insert the picture into the frame.

Tip

To insert a frame in a document, you also
can click the Frame button on the Word for
Windows 2.0 toolbar.

To import graphics stored on the Clipboard, choose the
Edit **P**aste command.

To import graphics from another program, you must
install the appropriate graphic import filter. If you
selected the Complete installation option, Word for
Windows installs all the graphic import filters.

To enclose a graphic in a border and draw horizontal
and vertical lines, choose the Format **B**order command.

To edit graphics, change colors, and insert callouts and text, click the Draw button on the toolbar, or choose any of the buttons from the Drawing toolbar.

Headers and Footers

Prints information, such as chapter headings, dates, or page numbers below the top margin or above the bottom margin of every page of a document. Header and footer information appears on-screen in Page Layout View and Print Preview.

To create a header or footer

1 Choose the View Header and Footer command.

Word switches into Page Layout mode. The Header/Footer toolbar appears. Outlined Header and Footer text entry boxes automatically appear at the top and bottom of the page.

2 Choose the Header or Footer from the toolbar (using the Switch Between Head and Footer button on the toolbar, the first button on the left).

3 Type the text for the header or footer in the appropriate text entry box.

4 Select the Switch Between Header and Footer button again to move to the other Header of Footer, if desired.

5 When finished, select the Close button on the Header and Footer toolbar.

> **Tip**
>
> You can include the current page number, date, or time in the header or footer by selecting a button from the toolbar.

See also *Numbering Pages*, *Print Preview*, and *View*.

Heading Numbering

Word 6 offers nine different levels of headings that can be used for structuring a document, numbered from 1 to 9. The numbering scheme used for those nine heading levels can be changed and modified, and Word for Windows Heading Numbering feature is the method by which it's done.

Heading numbering can be numeric, Roman numeral, lettered, or a combination thereof.

To select a heading numbering system

1 Choose the Format Heading Numbering command.

The Heading numbering dialog box appears. Six thumbnails are displayed, any of which can be selected for a default heading numbering scheme.

2 Click on a numbering thumbnail to select it and choose the OK button, or double-click on a heading numbering thumbnail to select it and return to the document.

To modify a heading numbering system

1 Select the Format Heading Numbering command.

The Heading numbering dialog box appears.

2 Click once on one of the six heading thumbnails to select it for modification.

3 Select the Modify command button.

The Modify Heading numbering dialog box appears.

The following options, checkboxes, and buttons are offered:

Option	Effect
Level	Scroll list box from which each level to be modified is selected.

continues

Option	Effect
Number Format	
Text Before	Specifies the characters to precede the numbering (a "(", for example).
Bullet or Number	List of various bullets or number formats that can be used for the Heading level.
Text After	Specifies the characters to follow the numbering (a ")" or a period, for example).
Font	Button, that when pressed, allows selection of another font for the heading.
Include from Previous Level	If a level 2-9 is selected from the Level list, this feature allows you to include the Numbers type, Numbers and Position, or nothing from the previous heading level.
Number Position	
Alignment of List Text	Specifies how the text of the Heading list will be aligned: Left, Right, or Centered.
Distance from Indent to Text	Specifies the space between the left Indent of the heading and the text of the list.
Distance from Number to Text	Distance between the Heading Numbering and the text of the list.
Hanging Indent	Checkbox enables a hanging indent if selected.

Option	Effect
Restart Numbering at Each New Section	Restarts heading numbering at each new section of the document.
Preview	Shows a preview of the heading format changes you make.

3 Since changing heading formatting can be fairly complex, use the Preview window frequently to check your work.

4 When finished, select OK or press Enter.

Help

The Word for Windows on-line Help system provides on-line, context-sensitive help for any function in Word for Windows. Help also enables you to learn to use basic and advanced Word for Windows features and the Word for Windows equivalents of WordPerfect commands. You can access Help at any time while you are working on a document.

The Help menu is divided into the following sections:

Section	Purpose
Contents	To view the Help contents
Search for Help on	To search for a specific topic
Index	Provides an index to help

To find a help topic

1 Choose the **Help Help Index** command.

The Help window appears.

2 To select a help topic by reading the Help Index, click the topic or press tab to highlight the topic and then press Enter. (Only underlined topics are available.)

You can use the vertical scroll bar in the Help window to display more help topics.

The following buttons and options are offered on the Help screen:

Search. Choose this button to find a help topic quickly. Type a topic in the text box at the top of the dialog box, and then choose the **S**how Topic button to display a list of topics in the box at the bottom of the dialog box. Choose the topic you want to read, and then choose the **G**o To button to display information on the topic.

Back. Choose this button to move to the preceding topic in the Help window.

<< (Browse Backward). Choose to move to the preceding topic within a series of related topics.

>> (Browse Forward). Choose to move to the next topic within a series of related topics.

Index. Choose to return to the Help Index.

History. Choose to display a list of the last 50 help topics. The History window displays a list of the last 50 help topics in the order you accessed them. To choose a topic you want to view again, double-click the topic or press ↓ or ↑ to highlight the topic and then press Enter.

File Print Topic. To print a help topic, choose this command from the Help window.

3 To return to the document, choose the **File Exit** command from the Help window.

To use "What Is" help

1 Press Shift+F1.

A question mark mouse pointer appears.

2 Position the question mark pointer on any menu command or part of the screen about which you want more information.

Command help	Provides more information about a command, choose the command.
Screen Element Help	For more information about a part on the screen, double-click the area of the screen.
Key Combination help	For more information about a key or key combination, press the key or key combination.

The information appears in the Help window.

Hyphenation

The Hyphenation option inserts a hyphen to divide a word that extends beyond the right margin of the page. The remainder of the hyphenated word wraps to the next line. Hyphenation can be turned on or off as desired. Hyphenation is used most often when using justified text in newspaper or uneven columns, to prevent excessive white space in a line of text.

To hyphenate words automatically

1 Position the insertion point at the beginning of the document or choose the text you want to hyphenate.

2 Choose the Tools Hyphenation command.

The Hyphenation dialog box appears, with the following options available:

Hyphenate CAPS	Choose this check box to hyphenate words in all uppercase letters if necessary.
Confirm	Choose this check box to confirm each hyphenation before the program divides the word.
Hot Zone	Choose an option from the Hot Zone list box to specify the *hyphenation zone*—the distance from the right margin within which the program hyphenates words. If you specify a lower number for the Hot Zone, more hyphens occur and the margins appear less ragged. If you specify a higher number for the Hot Zone, fewer hyphens occur and the margins appear more ragged.

3 Choose OK to begin hyphenation.

If you did not choose the Confirm option, Word for Windows hyphenates words automatically. If you selected the Confirm option, Word for Windows displays each suggested hyphenation in the Hyphenate At text box.

4 When Word for Windows displays a suggested hyphenation, choose Yes to hyphenate the word, No to skip the word, or Cancel to stop hyphenation.

or

Choose the Hyphenate At text box and change the hyphenation location.

If you began hyphenation at the beginning of the document or are hyphenating a section of text, Word for Windows displays the message Hyphenation is `complete` when it reaches the end of the document or section of text. Choose OK to return to the document.

If you began hyphenation in the middle of the document, Word for Windows displays the message `Do you want to continue hyphenation from the beginning of the document?` when it reaches the end of the document. Choose **Yes** to continue the hyphenation process at the beginning of the document or **No** to return to the document.

Indenting

Indenting aligns paragraphs relative to the margins. Indents can be either conventional or hanging indents, and they can be adjusted by specific measurements or by the Ruler.

To indent a paragraph

1 Position the insertion point in the paragraph you want to indent, or select the paragraphs you want to indent.

2 Choose the Format Paragraph command.

The Paragraph dialog box appears.

3 Choose the Indents and Spacing tab if its folder is not already displayed.

Option	Effect
Left	Enter a positive or negative number to align the entire paragraph to the right or left of the left margin.
Right	Enter a positive or negative number to align the entire paragraph to the left or right of the right margin.

continues

Option	Effect
Special indentation	Specifies whether the indent is to be a First Line indent or a Hanging indent.
First Line	Enter a positive number to indent only the first line of the paragraph.
Hanging	Enter a negative number to create a hanging indent.
None	Does not indent.
By	Specifies the distance of the indent in tenths of an inch. Use the up or down arrows to increase or decrease the value.

Shortcut

You also can use the ruler or click the Indent or Unindent command buttons on the toolbar to indent or "unindent" paragraphs quickly (see *Toolbar*).

Indenting is a perfect candidate for a macro. A macro enables you to automate the entire process described previously with a single keystroke. See *Macros* for more details.

See also *Format Paragraph*.

Index

The Index feature creates an index for a document. Word for Windows generates the page number references automatically. Word for Windows 6 makes the process of creating an index easier than ever by offering global index entry creation, easier formatting of indexes, Automarking capabilities, and more.

Index creation is essentially a two-step process. First, you must create index entries in your document. Then the index itself is created.

To create an index entry

1 Select the text (as many as 64 characters) you want to use as an index entry.

or

Position the insertion point where you want to create the index entry, type the index entry (as many as 64 characters), and then select the index entry you typed.

2 Choose the Insert Index and Tables command.

The Index and Tables dialog box appears.

3 Select the Mark Entry option button.

The Mark Index Entry dialog box appears. The text you originally selected appears in the Main Entry text box.

The Mark Index Entry dialog box has multitasking capabilities—that is, you can still work on the document while the dialog box is open.

4 The Mark Entry dialog box offers the following options:

Option	Effect
Subentry	This option is only required if you have subentries to the main Index entry— such as "sports" as a main entry and "baseball" as an indented subentry.

continues

Option	Effect
Range	Specifies a range of pages for an index entry. Bookmarks are used to provide the page range specification. See *Bookmark* for more details. You can also select the text whose page numbers you want in the entry, and create a bookmark using the Edit Bookmark command while the Mark Index Entry dialog box is still open.
Bold	Boldfaces index page numbers.
Italic	Italicizes page numbers.
Mark	Marks the Index entry.
Mark **A**ll	Marks all occurrences of the index entry.

5 Choose OK or press Enter to close the Index Entry dialog box and insert the index entry as hidden text.

> **Tip**
>
> To display the index entry codes in the document, click the Show/Hide button on the toolbar.

To manually format an index

1 Press Ctrl+Home to move to the end of the document.

2 Position the insertion point at the end of the document (after the last line of the text). You can press Ctrl+End to get there first.

3 To separate alphabetical sections with headings, press Ctrl+F9 to insert a set of brackets ({}) and then type any of the following field codes inside the brackets including the quote marks:

> ## Tip
>
> When you type field codes, you must type a space between the word **index** and the backslash (\), type a *separator code* (the letter after the backslash) to indicate the type of formatting (**h** indicates a heading, **e** indicates an entry separator, **l** indicates a list separator, **g** indicates a range separator, **s** indicates a sequence, and **d** indicates a sequence separator), type a space after the separator code, and enclose the separation information in quotation marks.

Field Code	Effect
{index \h "A"}	Separates sections {index \h "*a*"} with an upper- or lowercase letter.
{index \h "*characters*"}	Separates sections with the *characters* you specify (for example, -A-).
{index \h " "}	Separates sections with a blank line.
{index \h "¶ *A*"}	Separates sections with a blank line and a letter. Press Enter to type the paragraph mark.

4 To separate index entries from the page numbers, press Ctrl+F9 to insert a set of brackets ({}) and then type any of the following field codes inside the brackets:

Field Code	Effect
{index \e "→"}	Separates the index entry text from the page numbers with a tab. Press tab to type the tab symbol.
{index \l ";"}	Separates page numbers with a semicolon and a space (for example, 20; 35).
{index \g ":"}	Inserts a colon to indicate a range of page numbers (for example, 15:20).
{index \s chapter	Separates chapter \d "-"} and page numbers with a hyphen (for example, 15-20).

To compile an index

1 Use the Insert Index and Tables command to create the index entries and enter any formatting field codes.

2 Position the insertion point where you want the index to begin.

3 Choose the Insert Index and Tables command.

The Index and Tables dialog box appears.

4 Choose the Index tab, and the Index folder appears.

You can specify several types of index formats with the Formats list: Classic, Fancy, Modern, Bulleted, Formal, Simple, and Custom Style.

The Preview window displays a sample index with the respective format and index types.

5 The following options are available in the Index folder:

Option	Effect
Indented	Indents subentries to the left of the main entry.
Run-In	Sets subentries as a running sentence below the main entry.
Formats	Offers several default index styles: Classic, Fancy, Modern, Bulleted, Format, Simple, and Custom.
Preview	Displays a visual example of the selected index format.
Right Align Page Numbers	Aligns (justifies) the page numbers to the right margin.
Tab Leader	If Right Align is enabled, dotted tab leads and other types can be used to lead the eye from the entry to its page number.
Columns	Number of columns in Index, from 1 to 4.

6 Choose OK or press Enter to compile the index.

Word for Windows returns to the document, compiles the index, and then displays the index text and page numbers at the beginning of the document.

> **Shortcut**
>
> To do a quick and dirty index, you can select the text in your document, bring up the Index and Tables dialog, and select the Mark Entry button. Mark the entry or all instances of the entry. Complete this process for all desired index entries. After that's done, place the insertion point in the location of the document where you want the index, and reselect the Index and Tables dialog box. Press Enter. The index is generated.

Creating an Automark file for indexing

A *concordance* file must be created for Automarking index entries in a document. Concordance files are lists of text entries in a document from which an index is built.

To create an Automark file

1 Choose the File New command to begin a new document.

2 Choose the Table Insert Table command.

   Use a 2-column table, and as many rows as you think you need. Press Enter to create the table.

3 Type the text of the intended index entry exactly as it is in your *document*, including the uppercase or lowercase letters of the text.

4 Press tab. The cursor moves to the second column.

5 In the second column, enter the index entry text exactly as it should appear in the *index*. Press tab to go to the next row of the table.

6 Continue your index entries until the concordance is complete, and save the file as a normal document. (See *Save* for more details on saving your files.)

To use an Automark file for creating an index

1 Make sure that the insertion point is in the location of the document where you want the index to be placed

2 Open the document that you want to index; choose the Insert Index and Tables command. Make sure the Index folder is selected.

3 Choose the Insert Index and Tables command, and choose the Index tab if the folder is not already displayed.

4 Choose the AutoMark button.

The Open Index AutoMark File dialog box appears. It's similar in appearance to the File Open dialog box and functions the same way.

5 Choose the Automark concordance file and press Enter, or choose OK.

6 After the AutoMark file is opened, press Enter or choose the OK button in the Index and Tables dialog box.

The index is then generated.

Insert File

Insert File allows you to insert the entire contents of a document or text file into another document. The styles of the document being merged into are the styles that will be applied, so make sure that the styles of the two documents are compatible or that style compatibility isn't an issue when you perform this command.

To insert a file into an open document

1 Make sure the insertion point is located where the second file is to be placed in the current document.

2 Choose the Insert File command.

The File dialog box appears. It's the same as the File Open dialog box.

3 Choose the document file to insert into the current document. If the file is of a different format, you are prompted to select the type of file to Convert from.

4 Choose the OK button or press Enter.

> ## Reminder
>
> Only text and document files can be Inserted. Graphics files must be imported. See *Insert Picture* for more information.

Insert Object

Insert Object helps automate the Object Linking and Embedding process of integrating sound files, animations, small video clips, and pictures into your document. *Objects* are simply those data types—video clips, pictures, sounds, and so on—that add custom effects and offer a new dimension to your word processor files. Despite the esoteric term Object, there's really nothing exotic or unusual about them. Inserting Objects simply means that it is easier than ever to use different data types in your documents.

To insert an existing object into an open document

1 Make sure the insertion point is located where the object is to be placed in the current document.

2 Choose the Insert Object command.

The Object dialog box appears. Two tabs with folders are available: the Create New folder, and the Create from File folder.

3 Choose the Create from File tab, and the Create from File folder appears.

4 To locate the proper file, use the following options:

Option	Effect
File Name	Lists the files in the currently selected directory.
Directories	Choose the directory to search for the desired graphics file.
Drives	Choose the disk drive to search for the file you want.
Link to File	Creates an Object Link between the picture object and the document.
Display as Icon	Enables the picture data to be saved and embedded in the document (available only if the Link to File checkbox is selected), and displays the embedded object as an icon inside the document when it is displayed.

See *Link* for more detail on object linking and embedding.

> ## Tip
>
> If you have difficulty finding the desired file, you can choose the Find File option button. Assuming the file you select is created from a program that supports Objects (and not all Windows applications do, so be aware), choose the file name by highlighting it and pressing Enter, or double-clicking on the file name with the mouse.

5 When the file is found and selected, choose OK or press Enter. The dialog disappears and the Object is placed in the document at the location of the insertion point.

To create a new object for insertion into an open document

1 Make sure the insertion point is located where the object is to be placed in the current document.

2 Choose the Insert Object command.

The Object dialog box appears. Two tabs with folders are available: the Create New folder, and the Create from File folder.

3 Choose the Create New tab, and the Create New folder appears.

4 Choose from the following options:

Option	Effect
Object Type	Lists the object types currently supported in your system: for example, Microsoft Excel spreadsheets and graphs, PowerPoint presentations, and other applications programs in your system that support OLE in Windows.
Display as Icon	Enables the picture data to be saved and embedded in the document, and displays the embedded object as an icon inside the document when it is displayed.

5 Choose OK or press Enter.

The application program corresponding to the chosen Object type appears. The new object can now be created.

6 Create the new object.

> **Caution!**
>
> You can only create new objects in the
> other application: you cannot load files
> during the Create New process.

7 Choose File, Update in the program you are building
the object in; then quit the program to return to
Word. The object appears in your document.

> **Tip**
>
> Some application programs display a menu
> option, reading:
>
> ```
> Update and Return to FILENAME.DOC
> ```
>
> in which FILENAME.DOC is the name of the
> Word document where the Object is to be
> embedded. The option must be chosen
> before the object is embedded and the
> document updated.

See also *Link*.

Insert Picture

Insert Picture allows you to place pictures of many
different formats into your document. Over a dozen
graphics file formats are supported, including the
following:

File Extension	File Type
*.BMP	Windows Bitmap
*.CGM	Computer Graphics Metafile
*.DRW	Micrografx Designer/Draw
*.DXF	AutoCAD 2-D format
*.EPS	Encapsulated PostScript

continues

File Extension	File Type
*.HGL	Hewlett-Packard Graphics Language
*.PCT	Macintosh PICT
*.PCX	PC Paintbrush
*.PIC	Lotus 1-2-3 Graph
*.PLT	AutoCAD Plot
*.TIF	Tag Image File Format (TIFF)
*.WPG	DrawPerfect
*.WMF	Windows Metafile

To insert a picture into an open document

1 Make sure the insertion point is located where the picture is to be placed in the current document, or select the frame in which the picture is to be placed. (See *Frame* for more information on how to use frames to contain pictures.)

2 Choose the Insert Picture command.

The Insert Picture dialog box appears.

3 Select from any of the following options:

Option	Effect
File Name	Lists the files in the currently selected directory.
List Files of Type	Choose the file format type to list (*.PCX, *.TIF, for example).
Directories	Choose the directory to search for the desired graphics file.

Option	Effect
Drives	Choose the disk drive to search.
Link to File	Creates an Object Link between the picture object and the document.
Save Picture in Document	Enables the picture data to be saved and embedded in the document (available only if the Link to File checkbox is selected)
Preview Picture	Allows a thumbnail display of the picture in a Preview window in the Insert Picture dialog box.

For more information about linking files and saving pictures in a document, see *Link*.

4 To find your picture quickly, choose the picture format from the List Files of Type entry box.

5 Choose the file you want to insert from the File Name list.

6 Choose the drive and directory on which your picture file is located.

7 Choose OK or press Enter.

Italic

Italics are used to emphasize selected text. Italics can be applied to any scalable font available on your system.

Dialog box options can be used to set italic text, or a toolbar button can be used to save time.

To italicize text

1 Select the text to format for italics, or place the insertion point where you want to enter italicized text.

2 Choose the Format Font command.

3 Under the Font Style entry list, select Italic.

4 Choose the OK button or press Enter.

> **Shortcut**
>
> Press Ctrl+I or choose the Italics button on the Standard toolbar to skip steps 2-4.

Justify Text

Justifying is the process of aligning text to both left and right margins for a uniform appearance, as in newspaper columns.

To justify text in a document

1 Select the text to format for justification, or place the insertion point where your alignment of new text will begin.

2 Choose the Justify Paragraph button on the Formatting toolbar or follow the steps below:

3 Choose the Format Paragraph command.

4 Under the Alignment entry list, select Justified.

5 Choose the OK button or press Enter.

> **Shortcut**
>
> Choose the Justify Paragraph command button on the toolbar.

Tip

If parts of your text don't justify, it's possible that you have carriage returns inserted into your text. The best policy for text entry is not to use carriage returns within a paragraph, so that text formatting commands function properly.

Tip

To ensure smooth text justification without excessive white space on a line of text, make sure that Hyphenation is turned on. (See *Hyphenation* for more details.)

Labels

The Microsoft Word Envelopes and Labels feature creates mailing labels. You can print an address on a single label, or print a sheet of labels with the same address.

Before you can print labels, you should use a mailing label template to create a label format, and then create a new document file whose format is defined by the selected label type.

To create and print a sheet of labels

1 Choose the Tools Envelopes and Labels command. The Envelopes and Labels dialog box appears.

2 Choose the Label tab, and the Label folder appears.

3 Choose the Options button. The Label Options dialog box appears.

4 Set the following choices and settings under Label Options:

Option	Effect
Printer Information	
Dot Matrix	Enables proper printing of labels on a dot-matrix printer.
Laser	Enables proper printing of labels on a laser printer.
	The printer to be used must also be selected properly from Windows. (See your Windows 3.1 User Manual for more information on selecting and configuring your printer.)
Label Products	
Avery Standard	Avery Standard label type.
Avery Pan European	Avery European label type.
Other	Labels from other manufacturers
Product Number	Lists the various label types available under the Avery Standard or Pan European formats. The choices are dependent on the type of label selected.
Label Information	
Type	Shows the type of label selected.
Height	The height of the label in inches.
Width	The width of the label in inches.

Option	Effect
Page Size	The size of the page on which the labels are to be printed.

5 Choose Dot **M**atrix or **L**aser to specify the type of printer to use for label printing.

6 From the Label **P**roducts and Product Number list boxes, select the type of Avery or other brand mailing label to use, and the specific label type, respectively.

The Label Information display area shows the dimensions of the label type you have selected.

7 Choose the **D**etails option button. You can perform fine adjustments to your label for precise printouts and custom size labels.

The Custom Laser Information dialog box appears. (If you're printing labels to a dot-matrix printer, the same dialog box appears for dot-matrix.) The dialog box is dominated by a display showing a picture of the current label type. As measurements are changed, the label display changes to show the adjustments.

8 There are eight different measurement options that you can alter to create custom label measurements:

Option	Effect
Top Margin	Adjusts the top margin of the label.
Side Margin	Adjusts the side margin between labels.
Vertical Pitch	Adjusts the total amount of vertical space for the label.

continues

Option	Effect
Horizontal Pitch	Adjusts the total amount of horizontal space for the label.
Label Height	Adjusts the height of the label.
Label Width	Adjusts the width of the label.
Number Across	Number of labels in each row on the page.
Number Down	Number of labels down the page.

For all values, you can click the up or down arrows to increase or decrease the values for any label option.

Note the difference between Horizontal and Vertical pitch, and the height and width of the actual label. Pitch includes the spacing between labels as well as the width of the label.

8 When you finish the adjustments, select OK.

To create and print a single label

1 Choose the Tools Envelopes and Labels command.

The Envelopes and Labels dialog box appears.

2 Choose the Label tab, and the Label folder appears.

The next step is to select the label type. It determines the format of the document by which the labels are to be printed.

3 Choose the Options button. The Label Options button appears. The label options are the same as those described in the section about printing a sheet of labels.

4 Choose the Dot Matrix or Laser printer type.

5 Choose OK or press Enter.

6 Choose the Single Label option button. You can then specify the position of the label on the page by using the Row and Column entry boxes if you're using a laser-printed label. Dot-matrix labels cannot be adjusted.

7 Enter the address to be printed on the label sheet in the Address box.

8 Choose OK or press Enter.

The label prints.

> **Tip**
>
> To print a test label on plain paper, select the Only Check For Error command button (it looks like a check mark) from the Print Merge toolbar.

> **Shortcut**
>
> After you create a label format with the mailing label template, you can print sets of mailing labels by opening the main document that contains the label format and selecting the Tools Mail Merge command.

See also *Mail Merge*.

Line Spacing

Line Spacing isn't a menu option, but a short procedure. Word offers the ability to adjust line spacing and line height to improve the appearance of a document. Lines can be adjusted by point size, or by a number of lines, such as 1 1/2 or 2 lines, or as a specified value.

To adjust line spacing

1 Select the text for which you want to adjust line spacing, or place the insertion point where you want new text to be entered with a new line spacing value.

2 Choose the Format Paragraph command.

The Paragraph dialog box appears.

3 Choose one of the following spacing options:

Option	Effect
Before	Line spacing above each selected line, in point size.
After	Line spacing below each selected line, in point size.
Line Spacing	Auto specifies the line spacing automatically according to the tallest character on each line. Options for default line spacing include Single, 1.5 lines, Double, At Least (the current point size), Exactly, and Multiple Lines. Each type is described here:
Single	Specifies single spacing; adds no additional space between lines. Default.
1.5 Lines	Specifies 1 1/2 line spacing; adds 1/2 line of additional space between lines.
Double	Specifies double spacing; adds one line of additional space between lines.
At Least	Specifies the minimum amount of space between lines (Word for Windows adds additional space as needed).

Option	Effect
Exactly	Specifies a fixed amount of space between lines (Word for Windows does not add additional space, even if needed).
	At Least specifies the minimum amount of space between lines (Word for Windows adds additional space as needed). Exactly specifies a fixed amount of space between lines (Word for Windows does not add additional space, even if needed).
At	Specifies a customized amount of space between lines (in points or lines).

4 Choose OK or press Enter to adjust the spacing.

Shortcut

To adjust line spacing quickly, you can press Ctrl+1 for single spacing, Ctrl+5 for 1 1/2 line spacing, and Ctrl+2 for double spacing.

See also *Format Paragraph*.

Link

Word for Windows 6 offers enhanced capabilities for linking data from another application to a document. If you change the data in the other application, Word for Windows updates the linked data in the Word for Windows document. The process is called *Object Linking and Embedding (OLE)*.

Linking is the process of placing a copy of an object into a Word 6 document, or in multiple documents, and whenever the object is modified in the original application, all Word documents that contain the object, open or not, are automatically updated. But you cannot click on a linked object in Word to bring up the original application for editing. To transport a linked file, the document and all the separate files containing the linked object must be transferred as a group.

Embedding an object allows you to double-click on an object in Microsoft Word (a drawing or a chart, for example) and cause the original program that created the object to start up, displaying the object ready for editing. A single Word file with embedded objects can be taken to another computer without having to transport the separate Object files.

Word for Windows 6 supports OLE 2.0, which enables you to edit objects from different applications in the same window. Windows applications such as WinWord 6.0, the upcoming Microsoft PowerPoint 4.0 and Microsoft Excel 5.0, and future applications from other vendors can support OLE 2.0.

When using OLE 2.0, the Word menus and toolbars are temporarily replaced by those of the application that created the object. In a sense, a "super application" is created, in which one window can perform many different types of applications tasks—word processor to drawing program to presentation and back.

To create a link

1 Start the application and open the file that contains the data you want to link to a Word for Windows document.

2 Select the data you want to link.

3 Choose the **E**dit **C**opy command to copy the data to the Clipboard.

4 Switch to Word for Windows and go to the document in which you want to place the linked object.

5 Position the insertion point in the Word for Windows document in which you want to create the link.

6 Choose the **E**dit Paste **S**pecial command.

The Paste Special dialog box appears. Word for Windows highlights the default format in the **A**s list box.

7 If you do not want to use the format selected by Word for Windows, select a different format from the **A**s list box.

8 Choose the Paste **L**ink option button to create the link.

Windows inserts the linked data in the Word for Windows document.

To embed an object

1 Start the application and open the file that contains the data you want to link to a Word for Windows document.

2 Choose the **E**dit **C**opy command to copy the data to the Clipboard.

3 Bring up Microsoft Word and choose the **F**ile **O**pen command to open the document in which you want to embed the object.

4 Place the insertion point where you want to place the object.

5 Choose the **E**dit Paste **S**pecial command.

6 Choose the proper **A**s option (Microsoft Excel Chart Object, for example).

7 Choose the **P**aste option button to embed the object.

Tip

To edit the object, simply double-click on it and the original application program appears with the object. If the other application supports OLE 2.0, the Word 6 screen changes toolbars, menus, and window title to that of the new application.

> ## Tip
>
> OLE is a fairly complex procedure; Linking and Embedding are distinctly different methods of working with Objects. The Insert Object menu feature, described earlier in this book, may help ease the process of working with many different types of Objects and integrating them effectively into your document.

See also *Insert Picture* and *Insert Object*.

Macros

Macros record a sequence of keystrokes that you can play back later. Macros enable you to automate Word for Windows keystrokes, but not mouse actions. Since most Word operations are replicated in keystrokes as well as mouse commands, it's possible to assign macros to almost any action.

Macros can also be placed on a toolbar, a menu, or assigned a shortcut keystroke during the recording process.

To record a macro

1 Double-click the REC indicator on the status bar.

 The Record Macro dialog box appears.

2 In the **R**ecord Macro Name text box, type a file name for the macro or accept the default macro name.

3 Under the Make Macro **A**vailable To text box, select the document template (*.dot) that the macro should be available to. All Documents (Normal.Dot) is the default and usually the best option.

4 Type a description of the macro (as many as 255 characters) in the **D**escription text box. A description helps to explain exactly what the function of the macro is.

5 In the Assign Macros To section, choose one of the
three option buttons that are displayed:

Button	Effect
Toolbars	A new button is created on a toolbar after the macro is recorded.
Menus	Allows the placement of the macro on a menu after its recording.
Keyboard	Enables assignment of a keystroke to a macro after it is recorded.

The Customize dialog box appears, with the folder
displayed that corresponds to the macro recording
option you've selected: Toolbar, Menu, or Keyboard.

6 Choose OK or press Enter to record the macro.

REC appears on the status bar to indicate that you
are recording, and the mouse cursor changes to
show a small recording icon.

The Macro Record toolbar also appears, consisting
of two buttons from left to right: Stop and Pause.

7 Choose the Word for Windows menu commands and
perform the tasks you want to include in the macro.

Tip

If you commit an action during macro recording that you didn't intend, you can use
the Edit Undo command.

8 When you finish recording the macro, choose the
Stop button on the Macro Record toolbar.

To run a macro

Press the shortcut key combination for the macro, select
the button from the assigned toolbar, or select the
macro menu option.

or

1 Choose the T**o**ols **M**acro command.

The Macro dialog box appears.

2 Choose the macro you want to run from the **M**acro Name list.

3 Choose the **R**un button.

Tip

Macros can be edited directly using the WordBasic macro language. Instructions on doing so are included in the Microsoft Word Developer's Kit.

See also *Toolbar.*

Margins

At any position or page in your document, you can adjust the top, bottom, left, and right margins. The default for the top and bottom margin is one inch. The default for the left and right default margin is 1.25 inches. You can change the margin settings for either the entire document, or for the document pages from the current position of the insertion point. Margins can also be changed for a single paragraph for a single page.

To set margins by using the Page Setup command

1 Position the insertion point where you want to change the margins or select the text for which you want to adjust the margins.

2 Choose the **F**ile Page Set**u**p command.

The Page Setup dialog box appears, with four folders available: **M**argins, Paper **S**ize, **P**aper Source, and **L**ayout.

3 Choose the **M**argins tab, if the folder is not already displayed.

4 Set new values for any of the five different margins:

Margin	Effect
Top	Sets the top margin.
Bottom	Sets the margin at the bottom of the page.
Left	Sets the margin on the left side of the page.
Right	Sets the margin on the right side of the page.
Gutter	Sets the gutter width between pages (to allow, for example, for binding).

Other options include:

Option	Effect
From Edge Header	Adjusts distance of the Header from the top margin of the page.
Footer	Adjusts distance of Footer from bottom margin.
Preview	Displays adjustments to margins.
Mirror Margins	Checkbox option ensures congruent margins between left and right pages.
Apply To Whole Document	Applies margin adjustments to whole document.
This Point Forward	Applies adjustments from the current location forward.

5 Choose OK or press Enter to set the margins.

To set margins using the Ruler

1 Position the insertion point where you want to change the margins or select the text for which you want to adjust the margins.

2 Choose the **View Ruler** command if the Ruler is not already visible.

   The Ruler appears at the top of the document.

3 Choose the Margin Scale symbol ([) at the left end of the Ruler to display the margin markers ([ ]).

4 Drag the margin markers along the Ruler to set the new margins.

> **Tip**
>
> You can double-click the mouse above the tick marks on the Ruler to display the Page Setup Margins dialog box.

See also *Page Setup*, *Print Preview*, and *Ruler*.

Mail Merge

Word's Mail Merge feature combines two files into one file, inserting variable data into a fixed format.

Before you can merge files, you must create two files— the *data* file and the *main document* file. The data file contains the variable information, such as names and addresses, that you merge into the main document file. The main document file contains field names and the information that remains constant. Each field name corresponds to a field name in the data file. In the following examples a data file of addresses for batch mailing is created and then Mail Merge is performed. Also, database files in a variety of formats can be imported for merging operations.

The Word for Windows 6 mail merge process is somewhat lengthy and requires a little practice to master. Despite the large number of steps in the following examples, it's easier than it looks.

To create a data file and mailing labels

1 Choose the Tools Mail Merge command.

The Mail Merge Helper appears.

First, the Helper advises you to create a Main document for the merge process.

2 Choose the Create button. A list of documents to be created for the mail merge is pulled down, including the following options:

> Form Letters
>
> Mailing Labels
>
> Envelopes
>
> Catalog

With any of the four options, you are prompted to either create a new document or to use the current one for your data entry and merging.

3 Choose the Mailing Labels list option.

A dialog box appears, prompting:

```
To create the mailing labels, you can use the
active document window [your current document
name here] or you can create a new document
window.
```

4 Choose the New Main Document button. A new document appears in Microsoft Word.

5 Choose the Get Data button and select Create Data Source.

The Create Data Source dialog box appears. A list of field names is displayed in the Field Names in Header Row section:

> Title   Postal Code
>
> FirstName   Country

LastName   Home Number

Job Title   Work Number

Company

Address 1

Address 2

City

State

Tip

Each type of item in a data file (such as the
first name) is a *field*. All fields that belong
together (such as the name and address of
one person) are a *record*.

---

6 Click once on any field name to highlight it.

7 You can add custom fields by typing a name in the
Field Name text box and choosing the **A**dd Field
Name button to add it to the list.

8 Choose the **R**emove Field Name button if you want
to remove a selected field from the list.

9 Fields can be moved to different locations on the list
and placed in different order with the Move buttons
on the right side of the dialog box.

10 When your fields are organized as desired, select OK
or press Enter. The Save Data Source dialog box
appears.

11 Choose a directory in which to save the file, specify
a file name, and select OK or press Enter.

Since you've created a new file with no address
records, Word responds with the following message:

```
The data source you just created contains no
records. You can either add new records to your
data source by choosing the Edit Data Source
button or layout your main document by choosing
the Set Up Main Document button.
```

12 Choose the Edit Data Source button.

The Data Form dialog box appears. This is where you enter your address data, using the fields you just defined. Each data field has its own text box.

13 Enter the appropriate data in each field, and press tab to move to each subsequent field.

14 Click the Add New button to add a new record for data entry.

You can page through the records with the Record arrow buttons. The Find option button allows you to search for text in a specific record.

15 When finished entering records, select OK or press Enter.

16 Choose the Set Up Main Document button.

The Label Options dialog box appears.

17 After specifying the desired label format (see *Labels* for more information), choose OK or press Enter.

Selecting a label format is simple—all that's required is that you select the type of label—Avery address label, diskette label, and so on, and also the printer type to send the labels to—Laser or Dot Matrix.

The Create Labels dialog box appears.

18 A sample label template is shown in the Create Labels dialog box. To add fields to the blank label template, select the Insert Merge Field button and select each listed field as desired (FirstName, LastName, for example), one at a time, that should be on the template. Press Enter to add new lines in the template. Place a space between each field, as Word does not automatically separate fields.

19 Choose OK or press Enter. The Merge dialog box appears.

20 You can either Merge to a New Document or to the Printer. To test your merged documents for proper field placement, choose New Document.

21 Finally, choose the **M**erge button.

The label document is created.

When you close any of the documents, you are prompted to save the data file and label template document from which the labels are printed.

> **Tip**
>
> The data file you just created can be used for other Mail Merge purposes, such as envelopes, form letters, and catalogs.

To perform a mail merge for form letters

1 To begin, open the letter document you want to create as a form letter for the merge operation.

2 Choose the **C**reate option button in the Mail Merge Helper.

3 Choose the Form **L**etters list option.

4 A dialog box appears, prompting you to select either the Active Window (that holds the letter you wish to merge with) or to create a New Main Document. Choose the **A**ctive Window button.

The Helper then prompts you to select a data source for merging.

5 Choose the **G**et Data button, and then **O**pen Data Source.

The Open Data Source dialog box is functionally identical to the Open File dialog box.

6 Choose the data file containing your address records and select OK or press Enter.

If you haven't inserted Mail Merge fields into your form letter document, a dialog box appears with the message:

```
Word found no merge fields in your main docu-
ment. Choose the Edit Main Document button to
insert merge fields into your Main Document.
```

7 Choose the Edit **M**ain Document button.

The Mail Merge toolbar appears above your document.

8 Place the insertion point where you want to insert fields into your document—for example, in the TO: clause at the beginning of your form letter.

9 With the Mail Merge toolbar, choose the Insert Merge Field button.

A list of the data fields in your address document appears (FirstName, LastName, and so on).

10 For the TO: clause, for example, choose the FirstName field.

A FirstName field indicator is inserted into the document.

11 Press the space bar to place a space after the FirstName field.

12 Choose the Insert Merge Field button, and choose the LastName field.

13 Continue inserting fields where you deem appropriate.

14 Choose the Merge button on the Mail Merge toolbar.

15 You can either Merge to a New Document or to the Printer. To test your merged documents for proper field placement, select New Document. Merge Printer simply sends all your merged documents to the printer, which may turn out to be a huge waste of paper.

16 Choose the **M**erge button.

A new document created with all your fields inserted in each form letter. The file can then be saved or printed.

To perform a mail merge for envelopes

1 Choose the **T**ools Mail Merge command. The Mail Merge Helper appears.

2 Choose the **C**reate option button in the Mail Merge Helper.

3 Choose the **E**nvelopes list option.

Word displays the following message:

```
To create the envelopes, you can use the active
document window or a new document window.
```

4 Choose the **N**ew Main Document button.

Word displays a new document window.

5 Next, select the **G**et Data option button in the Mail Merge Helper, and then **O**pen Data Source.

The Open Data Source dialog box is functionally identical to the Open File dialog box.

6 Choose the data file containing your address records, and select OK or press Enter. (For information about creating an address database file for merging, see the section on Mailing Labels.)

Word displays the following message:

```
Word needs to set up your main document.
Choose the Set Up Main Document button to
finish setting up your main document.
```

7 Choose the **S**et Up Main Document button.

The Envelope Options dialog box appears.

8 Under Envelope Size, select the envelope type you wish to use.

Tip

You can also specify the font for both Delivery and Return addresses here. (See *Envelope* for more information.)

---

9 Choose OK or press Enter.

The Envelope Address dialog box appears, displaying a Sample Envelope Address template. This is where your address fields are placed to create the template.

10 To add fields to the blank envelope template, select the Insert Merge Field button and select each listed field as desired (FirstName, LastName, and so on), one at a time, that should be on the template. Press Enter to add new lines in the template. Place a space between each field, as Word does not automatically separate fields.

11 Choose OK or press Enter.

The Merge dialog box appears.

12 Choose the Merge command button or press Enter. After a moment, you'll see your merged documents, starting at the first page.

To perform a mail merge for a catalog

1 Choose the Tools Mail Merge command. The Mail Merge Helper appears.

2 Choose the Create option button in the Mail Merge Helper.

3 Choose the Catalog list option.

Word displays the following message:

```
To create the envelopes, you can use the active
document window or a new document window.
```

4 Choose the New Main Document button.

If you haven't inserted Mail Merge fields into your form letter document, a dialog box appears with the message:

```
Word found no merge fields in your main docu-
ment. Choose the Edit Main Document button to
insert merge fields into your Main Document.
```

5 Choose the Edit Main Document button.

The new document appears, with the Mail Merge toolbar appearing above it.

6 Place the insertion point where you want to insert fields into your document—for example, in the TO: clause at the beginning of your form letter.

7 With the Mail Merge toolbar, choose the Insert Merge Field button.

A list of the data fields in your address document appears (FirstName, LastName, and so on).

8 Choose a field to insert. For the TO: clause, for example, choose the FirstName field.

A FirstName field indicator is inserted into the document.

9 Press the spacebar to place a space after the field.

10 Choose the Insert Merge Field button, and select the LastName field.

11 Continue inserting fields where you deem appropriate.

> **Tip**
>
> To display the field codes in the main document, select the View Field Codes command.

12 Press Enter twice at the end of the field insertion to provide a blank line between catalog records.

13 You can either Merge to the New Document or to the Printer. To test your merged documents for proper field placement, select New Document.

14 Finally, choose the Merge command button or press Enter. The catalog listing is displayed on-screen.

> **Tip**
>
> Any record in your Merge databases can have fields in which no data is entered. For all the Mail Merge operations, a checkbox option is offered to prevent printing of blank fields. You can also enter as many fields in a record as you want, but each record in a data file must have the same number of fields (even if some fields are blank). The fields must be in the same order in each record.

Merge File

See *Insert File*.

Multilevel Lists

Word 6 offers capabilities for creating multilevel lists, which combine numbers, bullets and lettered references. Six basic styles are offered, and custom multilevel lists can also be created.

To create a multilevel list

1 Select the text to format for the list.

2 Choose the Format Bullets and Numbering command.

The Bullets and Numbering dialog box appears.

3 Choose the Multilevel tab, and the Multilevel folder appears.

4 Choose one of the six thumbnail styles displayed, or select the Modify option to change a list into a new format.

5 Choose OK or press Enter to apply the list format to the selected text.

See also *Bullets*.

Numbering Lines

Word offers the ability to automatically number lines in a document. Legal documents often require line numbering for readability and reference purposes. If you move lines, Word for Windows updates the line numbers to reflect the new line order.

To number lines

1 Position the insertion point where you want the line numbering to begin.

2 Choose the File Page Setup command.

The Page Setup dialog box appears, with four folders available: Margins, Paper Size, Paper Source, and Layout.

3 Choose the Layout tab, and the Layout folder appears.

4 Choose the Line Numbers option button.

The Line Numbers dialog box appears offering the following options.

Option	Effect
Add Line Numbering	Check box that enables or disables the line numbering.
Start At	Starts the line numbering at the specified line on the page.
From Text	Value adjusts the distance between line numbers and the text on the page.
Count By	Specifies increment between each line number (1,3,5...1,5,10... and so on).
Restart Each Page	Restarts line numbering at the top of each page.
Restart Each Section	Restarts line numbering at the beginning of each section.
Continuous	Numbers lines consecutively throughout the document.

5 Choose OK or press Enter to save the line number settings and close the Line Numbers dialog box.

6 Choose OK or press Enter again to insert the line numbers in the document.

To remove line numbers

1 Position the insertion point at the top left corner of the page where you want to begin removing line numbers.

2 Choose the File Page Setup command.

The Page Setup dialog box appears, with four folders available: Margins, Paper Size, Paper Source, and Layout.

3 Choose the Layout tab, and the Layout folder appears.

4 Choose the Line Numbers option button.

5 Deselect the Add Line Numbering check box (select the check box again to turn off the option).

6 Choose OK or press Enter to close the Line Numbers dialog box.

7 Choose OK or press Enter again to remove the line numbers.

Line numbers do not appear on-screen, but they do appear in the printed document. To see the line numbers in a document, select the File Print Preview command.

See also *Section Layout.*

Numbering Pages

Word offers a straightforward page numbering feature that automatically inserts page numbers and prints the page numbers in the position you specify. Automatic page numbering is a tremendously convenient feature that relieves the writer from having to manually enter and manage page numbers.

To number pages

1 Position the insertion point on the page where you want page numbering to begin.

2 Choose the Insert Page Numbers command.

The Page Numbers dialog box appears.

3 Select Top of Page or Bottom of Page to specify where you want the page number to print.

4 Select Left, Center, or Right to specify the alignment of the page number.

5 Choose OK or press Enter to number the pages.

To format page numbers

1 Follow the preceding steps 1-4 to create page numbering.

2 Choose the Format button.

The Page Numbers Format dialog box appears.

Several different page number formats can be specified: numeric page numbers, uppercase and lowercase alphabetic characters, and upper- and lowercase Roman numerals.

3 Chapter numbers can be included in the page numbers by selecting the Include Chapter Number check box.

4 If you include chapter numbers in your page numbering scheme, two other options are made available: Chapter Number Ends With and Use Separator.

Option	Effect
Chapter # Ends With	Specifies which header number in the current section the chapter number in the page numbering should end with.

Option	Effect
Use Separator	Offers several different types of separators between the chapter numbers and the page numbers.

5 When your page number format is chosen, select OK or press Enter.

6 Choose from the following options to position the page number:

Position

Header	Place page number in the header at the top of each page.
Footer	Place page number in the footer at the bottom of each page.

Alignment

Left	Aligns all page numbers with the left margin.
Right	Aligns all page numbers with the right margin.
Center	Places page numbers in the center.
Inside	Places page numbers on the inside margn of facing odd and even pages.
Outside	Places page numbers on the outside margin of facing odd and even pages.

7 Choose OK or press Enter to install page numbers.

Page numbers do not appear on-screen in Normal view, but print in the document. To see the page numbering in a document, select the View **P**age Layout or **F**ile Print Preview command.

Object Linking and Embedding

See *Insert Object* and *Link*.

Open

Opening is the process of opening a file in a document window. In many programs, it's also called loading a file. Word can have up to nine documents open at once. Files are opened from a disk drive on your system, or from another disk drive on a network.

To open a file

1 Choose the File Open command or press Ctrl+O or Ctrl+F12.

> **Shortcut**
>
> Choose the Open button on the toolbar (see *Toolbar*).

2 If the file you want to open is on another drive, select the drive name from the Drives list box.

3 If the file you want to open is in another directory, select the directory name from the Directories list box.

The list of files in the selected directory appears in the File Name list box.

4 Double-click the name of the file you want to open.

or

Press ↑ or ↓ to highlight the name of the file you want to open, and then press Enter.

> **Tip**
>
> Under the File menu, there's also a list of recently opened files, numbered in sequence. The Word default is four files. You can open any of those four files by choosing them. If you want to have a longer list of recently opened files, choose the **T**ools **O**ptions General folder and set a new number in the Recently Used File List (and make sure its check box is selected).

Outlines

Outlines can help you create basic structures upon which you build an outline of a document. If you move elements of the outline to another position in the document, Word for Windows renumbers the elements for you.

To create an outline

1 Position the insertion point where you want the outline to begin.

2 Choose the **V**iew **O**utline command.

   The Outline bar appears at the top of the document.

3 Type the text for the first heading and press Enter.

   Word for Windows inserts a first-level heading.

4 To type another heading in the document that is the same level as the preceding heading, type the text for the new heading and press Enter.

5 To enter a heading that is one level below the preceding heading (indented to the right of the preceding heading), you *demote* the heading level. A demoted heading level is sometimes called a *subordinate level*.

To demote a heading level, press Alt+Shift+←.

> ## Tip
>
> When you promote or demote a heading level, simply placing the cursor on the header line is sufficient—it isn't necessary to select the whole line.

6 To enter a heading level that is one level higher than the preceding heading (moved to the left of the preceding heading), you *promote* the heading level. A promoted heading level is sometimes called a *superior level*.

To promote a heading level, press Alt+Shift+← or click the Promote Heading Level button (the left arrow) on the Outline bar. Then, type the heading.

7 To enter body text after an outline heading, click the Demote to Body Text button on the Outline bar, or press Alt+Shift+5 (on the numeric keypad). Then type the text.

8 To move a heading up or down to another location in the Outline, select the heading to move, and click the Move Up or Move Down button, or press Alt+Shift+↑ or Alt+Shift+↓.

To display a sample outline and view the numbered levels, use the outline feature in a blank document.

Page Breaks

You can insert page breaks (where you want one page to end and another page to begin) in documents.

Word for Windows offers two kinds of page breaks—*soft* and *hard*. Whenever you fill a page of text, Word for Windows automatically inserts a soft page break (which appears on-screen as a dotted line). If you add or delete text, any soft page breaks move accordingly. To insert a page break in a specific location, you can manually insert a hard page break (that appears as a solid line).

Hard page breaks remain in the same location even if you add or delete text. They're often used at the ends of chapters to provide a clear break.

Hard page breaks can be treated almost as if they are just another character in your document—they can be inserted and deleted much like other characters.

To insert or delete a hard page break

To insert a hard page break, position the insertion point where you want to end one page and begin another and then press Ctrl+Enter.

To delete a hard page break, position the insertion point below the hard page break (the solid line) and then press Backspace.

To control page breaks within paragraphs

1 Select the paragraph(s) you don't want Word for Windows to break automatically with a soft page break.

2 Choose the Format Paragraph command.

The Format Paragraph dialog box appears.

3 Choose the Text Flow tab, and the Text Flow folder appears.

4 Choose one of the following Pagination options:

Option	Effect
Widow/Orphan Control	Prevents short words at the end of a paragraph from overlapping.
Keep Lines Together	Keeps all the lines of the paragraph on the same page.
Keep With Next	Keeps the paragraph and the next paragraph on the same page.
Page Break Before	Inserts a page break before the paragraph so that the paragraph appears at the top of the next page.

5 Choose OK or press Enter to return to the document.

Tip

To see the effect of the page breaks in a document, select the View Page Layout or File Print Preview command.

See also *Section Break*.

Page Setup

Word's Page Setup feature controls paper size and page orientation. You can specify different page sizes of up to 22 inches in height and 22 inches in width—large enough for a tabloid newspaper, for example.

To set or change the page setup

1 Position the insertion point at the beginning of the document for which you want to set the paper size or at the location where you want to change the paper size.

2 Choose the File Page Setup command.

The Page Setup dialog box appears, with four option folders available: Margins, Paper Size, Paper Source, and Layout.

3 Choose the Margins folder, if it is not already displayed, by clicking on its tab.

4 Change any of the options described in the following table:

Margin	Effect
Top	Sets the top margin.
Bottom	Sets the margin at the bottom of the page.
Left	Sets the margin on the left side of the page.

Margin	Effect
Right	Sets the margin on the right side of the page.
Gutter	Sets the gutter width between pages (to allow, for example, for binding).

5 Under the From Edge options, two different margin adjustments for headers and footers can be made:

Header	Adjusts the distance of the header from the top edge of the page.
Footer	Adjusts the distance of the header from the bottom edge of the page.

See *Header* and *Footer* for more details.

6 Choose the **S**ize & Orientation option button.

7 From the Paper **S**ize folder, select the paper size you want to use:

Paper Size	Description
Letter	8 1/2 by 11 inches (the default)
Legal	8 1/2 by 14 inches
Executive	725 by 10.5 inches
A4 (European)	210 by 297 millimeters
A5	148 by 210 millimeters
B5	184 by 257 millimeters
Envelope #10	4125 by 9.5 inches
Envelope DL	110 by 220 millimeters
Envelope C5	162 by 229 millimeters
Envelope Monarch	388 by 7.5 inches
Custom Size	

or

Specify a custom paper size by typing measurements in the **W**idth and **H**eight text boxes. The default unit of measurement is inches, but you can type **cm** to use measurements in centimeters.

8 In the Orientation section, select the Portrait or Landscape button to select the paper orientation.

9 Choose the **P**aper Source folder by clicking on its tab.

You may need to specify the paper tray that you are using in your printer, depending on whether you're printing regular pages or envelopes or other document paper types. Also, the **F**irst page of a document can be fed from a different paper tray than the **O**ther pages of the document.

A sample page appears in the Preview box.

10 Choose the **L**ayout folder by clicking on its tab. Different layout aspects can be specified:

Section Start	A section of the document can start in any of several places.
Different Odd and Even	Headers and footers can be designed to allow for facing pages
Different **F**irst Page	Allows a design for having no header or footer on the first page.
Verical Alignment	The document layout can be adjusted to Top, Centered, or Justified;
Line **N**umbers	Turns line numbering on and off in a document.

11 Choose OK or press Enter to set the Page Setup.

See also *Margins*, *Paper Orientation*, and *Headers and Footers*.

Paper Orientation (Portrait/Landscape)

For every document you create, you should set up your pages for vertical (portrait) or horizontal (landscape) layout and printing. The Page Setup command allows access to adjust the paper orientation of your document.

To change paper orientation

1 Choose the File Page Setup command.

   The Page Setup dialog box appears.

2 Click on the Paper Size tab and its folder appears.

3 Under Orientation, select the Portrait or Landscape button. The Orientation thumbnail display and the Preview display change the paper orientation to reflect the Portrait or Landscape mode.

4 Choose OK or press Enter.

Password Protection

Word offers a password document protection feature. The process of assigning a password to a document is straightforward, but it's important to keep written records of the files and their assigned passwords, particularly in a networked environment. Two different passwords can be assigned: an overall Protection password, in which the file simply cannot be opened unless the password is correctly issued; and a Write Reservation password, that allows the file to be read in Microsoft Word for Windows, but not written to.

> ## Caution!
>
> Use passwords with caution. Word for Win-
> dows does not open a password-protected
> file unless you enter the correct password.

To set a password

1 Choose the File Save As command or press F12.

2 If you have not named the document, type a name in
the File Name text box.

3 Choose the Options button.

The Save folder in the Options dialog box appears.

4 There are two File Sharing options displayed at the
bottom: in the Protection Password text box, type a
password (of as many as 15 characters, including
spaces, in upper- or lowercase letters). For the
Write Reservation Password, do the same if desired.

> ## Caution!
>
> It's better not to use easily guessed pass-
> words (such as your last name, or your
> birthday). Also, keep a written record of the
> passwords you create along with the files to
> which they're attached.

The password or passwords appear as a series
of asterisks.

5 Choose OK or press Enter to enter the password(s).

The Confirm Password dialog box appears.

6 In the Reenter Protection Password text box, type
the password again (to verify it).

The password appears as asterisks again.

7 Choose OK or press Enter again to return to the
Save As dialog box.

8 Choose OK or press Enter (in the Save As dialog box) to save the document with password protection.

To remove a password

1 Choose the File Save As command or press F12.

2 Choose the Options button.

The Save folder in the Options dialog box appears. The password appears as a series of asterisks. Type in the password again.

3 Press Del to delete the password.

4 Choose OK or press Enter to save the change and return to the Save As dialog box.

5 Choose OK or press Enter (in the Save As dialog box) to save the document without password protection.

See also *Save/Save As*.

Paste

The Paste command allows you to Insert the Clipboard's contents into another location in the same document, into another document, or into a document in another Windows program.

To paste data

1 Select the text you want to paste elsewhere.

2 Cut or copy the data to the Clipboard (see *Cut* or *Copy*).

3 If you want to paste the data elsewhere in the current document, scroll and place the insertion at the desired location for the paste. If you want to paste the data to another document (or to a document in another Windows program), choose Window, then select the document where you want to paste data.

4 Position the insertion point where you want to insert the Clipboard's contents.

5 Choose the **E**dit **P**aste command or press Ctrl+V.

A copy of the Clipboard's contents appears in the document. The data also remains on the Clipboard until you cut or copy something else or exit Windows.

Tip

To choose the Cut, Copy, or Paste command quickly, you can click the Cut, Copy, or Paste button on the toolbar.

Caution!

Be careful when pasting—only the last data copied can be pasted.

See also *Clipboard*, *Copy*, *Cut*, and *Toolbar*.

Paste Special

The Paste Special command allows you to insert the Clipboard's current contents into another location in a Word document, and to set the pasted item's status as an OLE object to be linked or embedded. The process is also called executing a Paste-Link.

To paste-link data from the clipboard

1 Open the application program containing the information you want to paste as an Object.

2 Cut or copy the data to the Clipboard (see *Cut* or *Copy*).

3 Switch to Word for Windows and position the insertion point where you want to insert the Clipboard's contents.

4 Choose the **E**dit Paste **S**pecial command.

The Paste Link dialog box appears.

5 Choose the file type to be pasted from the Clipboard from the **As** entry list.

6 Choose the pasting method from one of the two buttons on the left:

Button	Effect
Paste	Allows a conventional paste of data from the clipboard.
Paste **L**ink	Allows an Object Link to be created, so that whenever the Pasted object is modified in its original application, the changes will be reflected in your Word document.
Display as Icon	Displays the OLE pasted object as an icon in your document. The reader can then double-click on the icon in order to view the object.

7 Choose OK or press Enter to execute the Paste Link and return to your document.

See also *Insert Object*, *Insert Picture*, *Clipboard*, *Copy*, *Cut*, and *Toolbar*.

Print Preview

Print Preview displays on-screen what the document will look like when printed. If your monitor can display graphics, graphics also appear in the preview. Print Preview is a very useful feature for checking layouts and how a document will print out before you actually print it. It's a time-saver and can save paper, too.

You can perform basic editing in Print Preview.

To preview a document

1 Position the insertion point in the page where you want to begin the document preview.

2 Choose the File Print Preview command.

The Print Preview screen appears.

3 Click once inside the document. The mouse cursor will change to a Zoom tool. Click again to view the document more closely. Click again to zoom back out.

There are a series of buttons on the Print Preview bar. They perform the following options, from left to right:

Print	Sends the document to the printer.
Magnifier	Offers a single-level zoom, as with clicking inside the document.
One Page	Enables single-page view.
Multiple Pages	Enables print preview of up to six pages at a time on the screen.
Zoom Control	Offers control of Zoom view percentages.
View Ruler	Enables view of the Ruler, showing tabs and measurements.
Shrink to Fit	Offers the ability to remove orphans and widows—to eliminate lagging single lines on a page.
Full Screen	Enables Full Screen view.
Close	Leaves Print Preview and returns to the Word screen.
Help	Print Preview Help.

4 To change the page view, select the Multiple Pages button on the Preview bar.

5 To switch back to page view, select the **Margins** button again.

See also *Margins*, *Print*, and *View*.

Print Setup

With the Print Setup option, you can choose a printer, switch printers, change printer settings, select cartridges and fonts, and select a paper source. The printer being chosen must also be properly selected and set up within Windows. Word's Print Setup feature is necessary for selecting different paper sources, or to ensure that a different printer can be selected and used properly.

To select a printer

1 Choose the **File Print** command.

The Print dialog box appears.

2 To change printers, choose the Printer button.

The Print Setup dialog box appears.

3 From the list of installed printers, select the printer you want to use.

If you want to use another printer that is not on the list, you will need to use the Windows Control Panel Printers facility to install the proper printer drivers and configure it for use under Windows and Word.

To change printer settings

1 Choose the File Print Setup command.

2 To change printer settings, choose the **O**ptions button.

The Options dialog box appears. The settings in the dialog box can vary according to the printer selected, but for most laser printers dithering and intensity control are the key settings. A slider bar is

provided to adjust each value. Dithering adjusts
the appearance of grays in a picture and intensity
darkens or lightens the picture. It may take a few
printouts to get it right.

3 Choose OK or press Enter to go back to the Print
Setup dialog box.

4 Choose the Close button or press OK to return to
the Print dialog box.

5 Choose the Options button.

The Options dialog box appears, with the Print
folder displayed.

The following options are offered for printing
documents:

Option	Effect
Include with Document	
Summary Info	Prints summary info with the document.
Field Codes	Prints field codes within the document.
Annotations	Prints annotations along with the document.
Hidden Text	Prints hidden text with the document.
Drawing Objects	Prints any drawing objects included in the document.
Printing Options	
Draft output	Allows faster printing with lower quality.
Reverse Print	Prints pages last to first.
Order Update Fields	Updates Mail Merge fields if necessary.
Update Links	Updates OLE links to other applications after printing.

Option	Effect
Background Printing	Allows background printing as you're performing other tasks.

Change the settings and then select OK or press Enter to accept the settings and return to the Print Setup dialog box.

6 Choose OK or press Enter to accept the printer selection and setup and return to the document.

> **Tip**
>
> Many printer settings must be changed from within Windows, in the Control Panel.

See also *Print*.

Print

Word offers easy printing of a document using the printer and font settings you select. Single pages, page ranges, and disconnected pages or page ranges can be printed. Copies can also be collated as you print.

To print a document

1 Open the document you want to print.

2 Choose the **F**ile **P**rint command or press Ctrl+P, or Ctrl+Shift+F12.

The Print dialog box appears.

3 Choose from the following printing options:

Option	Effect
Page Range	
All	Prints all pages in the document.

continues

Option	Effect
Current Page	Prints current page.
Pages	Allows printing of a single page, a range of pages, or disconnected groups and ranges of pages: (1, 3-5, 10, 11-20).

Print

All Pages in Range	Prints all pages in the specified range.
Odd Pages	Prints only odd pages in the document.
Even Pages	Prints only even pages in the document.

Print What

Document	Prints the document.
Summary Info	Prints the summary information about the current document—word count, file size, and so on.
Annotations	Prints annotations to the current document.
Styles	Prints the styles for the current document—their construction and setup.
Auto Text entries	Prints the AutoText entries for the current document.
Key Assignments	Prints the keystroke assignments used in Microsoft Word.
Print to File	Prints the document to another file.

Option	Effect
Collate Copies	Prints a complete copy of the document before the next copy of the document begins to print. If you select the Collate Copies, Word for Windows creates the specified number of copies, and then sends all the copies of the document to the printer. This option produces collated copies, but printing takes longer.

4 Choose OK or press Enter to print the document.

Shortcut

To print a document immediately (without going through dialog boxes), click the Print button on the Toolbar.

Tip

You can set print defaults for all Word for Windows documents by using the Tools Options command.

See also *Find File*, *Print Preview*, and *Print Setup*.

Repeat

The Repeat function executes the last command, action, or text you typed. You can use this feature to apply complex character and paragraph formats to text, perform searches, and duplicate text in a long document.

To repeat a command, an action, or typing

Choose the **E**dit **R**epeat command or press F4.

See also *Undo*.

> **Tip**
>
> Macros are also a good way to automate or repeat commands. See *Macro*.

Revision Marks

Revision marks indicate when, where, and by whom changes in a document have been made. They indicate changes to a document by displaying revision bars in the margins and by using underlined characters for inserted text, and strikethrough characters for deleted text.

Revision marks are a useful tool for keeping close track of changes in a document. They're especially handy if several people are working on the same document, because each user's revisions are shown in a different color on-screen.

Word for Windows uses the Revision Marks options you set to compare an edited document to the original document when you compare versions (see *Compare Versions*).

To display revision marks

1 Open the document in which you want to mark changes.

2 Choose the **T**ools Re**v**isions command.

The Revisions dialog box appears.

3 Choose **M**ark Revisions While Editing.

4 To make revisions visible in the document while you work, select the Show Revisions on **S**creen check box. If you want to hide revision marks but want to track changes during your work with the document, disable the Show Revisions on **S**creen check box.

5 To show revision marks in a printout, select the Show Revisions in **P**rinted Document check box.

To use revision marks

1 Add new text to the existing text in your current document.

The text you add has the character format you specified in the Revision Marks dialog box (the default is Underline). Also, the Mark Revisions While Editing check box, in the Revisions dialog box, should be enabled.

2 Delete text by selecting the **E**dit Cu**t** command, pressing Del, or clicking the Cut button on the Toolbar.

The text you delete changes to strikethrough characters.

To review revision marks

1 Two versions of the same document can be compared with the Compare Versions option button. The other version of the current file to be compared is loaded into Word just as any other file is.

2 The Review Revisions dialog box appears. To ensure a smooth continuous movement through revisions in the document, select the Find Next after Accept/Reject check box.

3 To begin reviewing revisions, click on one of the Find buttons.

4 To accept a revision, choose the **A**ccept button.

5 To reject a revision, choose the **R**eject button.

6 To end your review session, select the Cancel button or press Escape.

> **Tip**
>
> You can merge two versions of the same document with the Merge Revisions option button. The file to be merged with the current document is loaded from the file requester dialog box.

To customize revision marks

1 Choose the Tools Revisions command.

The Revisions dialog box appears.

2 Choose the Options button.

The Revision Options dialog box appears.

3 Imported text can be set up for Bold, Italic, Underline, or Double Underline, and any of 16 colors available under Windows can be assigned to imported text. The same is true for Deleted text.

4 Choose OK or press Enter to return to the Revisions dialog box, and Enter again to return to the document.

Ruler

The Ruler is a handy and powerful graphical tool which allows you to change character and paragraph formats quickly. You can use the Ruler to set tabs and margins, format text, and adjust columns and tables.

To display or hide the Ruler

- To display the Ruler, select the View Ruler command.

- To hide the Ruler, select the View Ruler command again.

To set or change a tab

1 Select the text for which you want to set or change tabs or position the insertion point where you want the new tabs to begin.

2 To set a new tab, click the Ruler where you want to add the tab. The tab marker, a black right-angled line, indicates the position of the tab. The direction of the bottom leg of the *L* indicates whether the tab is a left or right tab. If the bottom leg crosses on both sides, it's a center tab.

- To adjust the position of an existing tab, drag the tab marker to the new position.

- To delete an existing tab, drag the tab marker off the Ruler and release the mouse button.

- To change the type of tab, delete the existing tab, and then click the Ruler where you want to add the tab.

To reset the left and right margins

1 Click and hold the margin boundary marker at the left end of the Ruler.

2 Drag the margin markers to the new positions.

To indent paragraphs

1 Select the paragraphs you want to indent, or place the insertion point where you wish to indent new text.

2 Perform the following ruler adjustments for various indents:

To indent an entire paragraph	Drag the small box at the left end of the ruler to the right. The box and triangle indent markers will all move.
To indent only the first line	Drag the first-line indent markers (the top triangle at the left end of the ruler) to a new position.

To create a hanging indent (first line hanging beyond the rest of the paragraph)	Drag the left indent marker (the triangle just above the box or the left end of the ruler) to the right. The box will move with it, and the paragraph will acquire a first-line hanging indent.
To left indent the selected paragraph (indent the paragraph's right margin to the left)	Drag the right indent marker (the triangle at the right end of the ruler) to the left.

To adjust column width

Before you can adjust column width on the Ruler, you must use the Format Columns command to set up the columns.

1 Click the margin scale symbol ([) at the left end of the Ruler.

2 Drag the column markers ([and]) to the new positions.

To adjust column width for a table

1 Select the table rows for which you want to adjust the column width.

2 The following adjustments can be made on the Ruler for column width adjustments and text indenting within columns:

To adjust a column width without adjusting the width of the table	Click and hold the table column boundary marker (a square series of dots at each column margin on the ruler) and drag it to its new position.

To adjust a column width and the width of the entire table | Hold the Ctrl+Shift keys down as you adjust the column boundary markers.

Tip

While column adjustments can be done on the Ruler, the process is imprecise and can be frustrating. To employ more precise column adjustments, use the Table Cell Height and Width menu command.

Also note that text in table cells, rows, and columns can be indented, in the same way as regular text paragraphs, on the ruler.

See also *Columns*, *Format Paragraph*, *Margins*, *Toolbars*, *Tables*, and *Tabs*.

Save/Save As

Microsoft Word's Save/Save As feature allows you to store a new or existing document on disk. You can use the Save As command to save a file under a different name, to save as a different word processor format, and to save a file to a different drive and/or directory.

Saving a document in a different format allows other word processors and other applications to send your document to others for viewing and editing.

To save a document

1 Choose the File Save or the File Save As command, or use any of the key sequences below:

Save	Ctrl+S
	Alt+Shift+F2
	Shift+F12
Save As	Alt+F2
	F12

If you are saving a document you have saved previously, and you selected the File Save command, Word for Windows saves the document.

If you have not saved the document previously or you selected the File Save As command, the Save As dialog box appears.

2 To name the document or to save the document with a different name, type the name in the File Name text box.

If you have saved the document previously, the current name is selected in the File Name text box. To save the document with a new name, simply type the new name.

3 The following options for saving files are also offered:

Option	Effect
Drives	List box to save the file to a different disk drive.
Directories	List box to save the file to a different directory.
Save File As Type	List box of different file formats to save the file as: WordPerfect, Microsoft Works for Windows, Word for Windows 2.0, Ami Pro, and others.

Documents can also be saved as a Template, so that future documents can be created using the same styles, margin and page settings, and so on.

4 Choose OK or press Enter to save the new file.

The File Save command replaces the original copy of a document (the file on your drive) with the document on-screen. The File Save As command enables you to rename the document on-screen so that you can retain the earlier version as well as save your changes.

If you try to close a document without saving it, Word for Windows asks whether you want to save the document.

You also can click the Save button on the Toolbar rather than selecting the File Save command (see *Toolbar*).

See also *Convert File*.

Section Breaks

Section breaks (where you want one section to end and another section to begin) can be inserted in long documents to denote sections for organization and formatting purposes. Sections can be a single paragraph long or can stretch for many pages. Sections are created when you want to change different elements in part of a document, including margins and page setup, columns, page number formatting and positioning, headers and footers, and other elements.

To insert a section break

1 Position the insertion point where you want the new section to begin.

2 Choose the Insert Break command.

The Break dialog box appears.

3 Choose one of the following types of section breaks:

Option	Effect
Next Page	Begins the new section at the top of the next page.
Continuous	Begins the new section on the same page as the preceding section without inserting a page break.
Even Page	Begins the new section at the top of the next even-numbered page.

continues

Option	Effect
Odd Page	Begins the new section at the top of the next odd-numbered page.

4 Choose OK or press Enter to insert the section break.

A section break mark (a double line) divides the document into sections.

To delete a section break

Position the insertion point below the section break mark (the double line) and press *Backspace*.

Tip

The status bar indicates the current section (the section that contains the insertion point).

See also *Headers and Footers, Margins, Numbering Lines, Numbering Pages, Page Breaks, Page Setup,* and *Section Layout.*

Section Layout

Word's Section Layout features help you specify the beginning of a section, vertical alignment (how the top of the section aligns with the top margin), and other options. As mentioned in *Section Break*, sections are created when you want to change the formatting of part of a document. A headline for a newsletter could be its own section, and a set of three columns of text under the headline could be another section. In long documents, an index could be a section by itself, with a different header, footer, and page numbering scheme.

To format a section

1 Position the insertion point in the section you want to format.

2 Choose the Format Section Layout command.

The Section Layout dialog box appears.

3 From the Section Start list box, select one of the following options:

Option	Effect
New Page	Begins the new section at the top of the next page.
New Column	Begins the new section at the start of the next column.
Continuous	Begins the new section on the same page as the preceding section without inserting a page break.
Odd Page	Begins the new section at the top of the next even-numbered page.
Even Page	Begins the new section at the top of the next odd-numbered page.

4 From the Vertical Alignment list box, select one of the following options:

Option	Effect
Top	Aligns the first line with the top margin.
Center	Centers text between the top and bottom margins.

continues

Option	Effect
Justified	Expands the space between paragraphs to align the first line with the top margin and last line with the bottom margin.

5 Other Section Break options include:

Option	Effect
Suppress Endnotes	Prevents the printing of any endnotes at the end of the section
Line Numbers	Command button allows enabling of line numbers and to specify line numbers layout (see NUMBERING LINES for more information).

6 Choose OK or press Enter to save your choices and return to the document.

Tip

You can also double-click the section break mark (the double solid line) at the top of the section to display the Section Layout dialog box.

See also *Headers and Footers*, *Margins*, *Numbering Lines*, *Numbering Pages*, *Page Breaks*, *Page Setup*, and *Section Breaks*.

Spelling

Word 6 enables fast and easy spell checking in a document. You also can use the Spelling feature to check a selected word or to find capitalization errors and duplicate occurrences of a word (such as **the the**). Custom dictionaries can also be loaded and used for special documents.

Custom dictionaries are useful for medical, legal, and technical documents to ensure accuracy when spell-checking arcane terms for documents in those fields.

To check spelling

1 Position the insertion point where you want to begin checking spelling or select the text you want to check.

2 Choose the Tools Spelling command or press F7.

The Spelling dialog box appears. Word for Windows displays the first unmatched word in the Not in Dictionary text box.

3 Choose one of the following options for the unmatched word:

Option	Effect
Ignore	Does not change the word.
Ignore All	Does not change any occurrence of the word.
Change	Changes the word to the word you type in the Change to text box.
Change All	Changes all occurrences of the word to the word you type in the Change to text box.
Add	Adds the word to the dictionary.
Auto Correct	Enables auto correction feature for any further occurrences of the currently selected word.

continues

Option	Effect
Undo Last	Undoes the preceding correction (up to five corrections).
Suggest	Displays a list of proposed corrections in the suggestions box. Choose the correct word from suggestions list and then select Change or Change All.
Cancel	Exits the Spelling feature.
Options	Changes Spell Checking options (see next section).
Delete	Deletes the duplicate occurrence of the word.

Tip

Leave the Always Suggest check box off in the **Tools Options** Spelling folder if you don't want to spend time using suggestions.

After you select an option, Word for Windows finds the next unmatched word. When Word for Windows reaches the end of the document or selected text, a dialog box appears.

4 If you began checking spelling at the beginning of the document, select OK or press Enter to return to the document.

Or, if you began checking spelling in the middle of the document, select **Yes** to check the remainder of the document or select **No** to stop checking.

To change spell checking options

1 Choose the **Tools Options** command.

2 Choose the Spelling tab.

3 Select from any of the options for changing Spelling functions:

Option	Effect
Suggest	
Always	Check box enables consistent suggestions if applicable.
Suggest From **Main** Dictionary Only	Spelling suggestions from the Main dictionary only.
Ignore	
Words In UPPERCASE	Changes the word to the word you type in the Change to text box.
Words with Numbers	Changes all occurrences of the word to the word you type in the Change to text box.
Custom Dictionaries	
New	Allows creation of a new dictionary.
Edit	Enables editing of the selected dictionary as a Word document.
Add	Add another dictionary to the custom dictionary list.
Remove	Remove a dictionary from the list.
Other option	
Reset Ignore All	Resets the list of words to ignore during a spell check to zero

Spike

The Spike is an electronic equivalent of the old-time
editor's Spike, where notes, tips, and miscellaneous bits
of information were stored by punching the paper over
a sharp spike. The Word 6 Spike inserts a collection of
frequently used text and graphics into a document, in a
last-in-first-out fashion. The Spike functions in a similar
way to the Glossary. You can use the Spike to collect
text and graphics from one or more documents and then
insert the contents of the Spike into another location.
The Spike enables a batch cut-and-paste of several
elements without having to go through a laborious
series of operations.

To collect text or graphics by using the Spike

1   Select the text or graphic you want to store by using
the Spike.

Caution!

The amount of text and graphics or other
elements you can store depends on your
computer's available memory.

---

2   Press Ctrl+F3 to copy the text or graphic and store it
in the Spike. The selected text or graphics will be
deleted from the page.

3   Repeat steps 1 and 2 to add text or graphics on
"top" of the text or graphics currently stored in the
Spike.

To insert the contents of the Spike

1   Position the insertion point where you want to
insert the contents of the Spike.

2   Type **SPIKE**.

3   Press F3.

Word for Windows inserts a copy of all the text or
graphics stored in the Spike.

To empty the Spike

1 Position the insertion point where you want to insert the contents of the Spike.

2 Press Ctrl+Shift+F3.

Word for Windows inserts all the text or graphics stored in the Spike and empties the Spike.

Starting Word for Windows

Starting Word for Windows is straightforward. Here's how to start up the Word for Windows program:

To start Word for Windows

1 At the C:> prompt, type **WIN** and press Enter to start Windows.

The Windows Program Manager appears. The Word for Windows 2.0 group window contains the Word for Windows icon.

2 Double-click the Word for Windows icon.

Word for Windows starts and displays a new, blank document window.

To start Word for Windows with a document

Use drag and drop to move files into a Program Manager group.

1 From inside Windows, start the Windows File Manager.

2 Choose a drive and directory that contains document files created with Word for Windows 6.

3 Click once on a Word 6 document file to select it, and hold the mouse button down.

4 Drag the file name from the Program Manager to a Windows group in Program Manager (the mouse cursor will change to show a small file icon attached to it).

The file, when dragged to the group, displays a Word 6 icon.

5 Double-click on the file icon. Word 6 will start up and display the document file for editing.

> **Tip**
>
> You can also double-click on the file name in File Manager to open the file directly into Word.

Styles

Styles are one of Word's most powerful and useful features. Styles allow fast and efficient formatting of complex documents.

You can define a group of paragraph and character formats as a *style* and save the styles you define in a *style sheet*, which is a list of styles that are part of a document or document template.

Styles are an excellent way to save work and time spent formatting text over and over by hand. Style creation also ties together almost every character and paragraph formatting feature Word 6 has to offer.

To create a style

1 Choose the Format Style command.

The Style dialog box appears.

The Style dialog box is split up into several sections:

Paragraph	Displays the effects of the created or selected style on a sample paragraph.
Preview Character	Displays the typeface used in the style.
Preview Styles	Lists the styles available in the document.

| Description | Displays the syntax description of the style. |

2 Choose the **New** button.

The New Style dialog box appears.

3 Type in a name for the new style in the **Name** text box.

4 Two different Style **Types** can be defined: Paragraph, or Character. Choose Paragraph.

5 The **Based On** text box displays the style which the new one to be created is presently based upon. The new style you're creating has the characteristics of the style listed there. To change this, scroll down the list until the style you wish to base the new one on is highlighted, and press Enter.

The Preview window in the New Style dialog box will adjust to show the different style.

6 Choose (and hold) the **Format** pop-up button. A pull-down list offers the various formatting options. Choose any of those options to bring up a corresponding dialog box.

Option	In the Dialog
Font	Specify any character formats and line spacings for the style. For more information, see *Font*.
Paragraph	Specify any paragraph formats for the style. For more information, see *Format Paragraph*.
Tabs	Specify any tab settings for the style. For more information, see *Tabs*.
Border	Specify any borders, boxes, and shading or shadows for the style. For more information, see *Format Borders and Shading*.

Option	In the Dialog
Language	Specify the language to be used in a multilingual document.
Frame	Specify any frame type, text wrap, frame size, and horizontal and vertical positioning for the frame in the style. For more information, see *Frames*.
Numbering	A bulleted list or numbered list style can be defined (see *Bullets* for more details).

7 Make sure your style is named the way you want it.

8 If you want to use your new style in new documents as well as the current one, select the Add to Template check box.

9 Repeat steps 3 through 9 to create or edit other styles.

10 Choose the OK button or press Enter to close the Style dialog box and return to the document. Your new styles will be available to the document.

To edit a style

Editing styles is done using most of the same methods as creating a new style.

1 Choose the Format Style command.

The Style dialog box appears.

2 In the Styles list, select the style you wish to change.

3 Choose the Modify button.

The Modify Style dialog box appears. The style Name will be displayed.

4 The **B**ased On text box displays the style which the new one to be created is presently based upon. The new style you're creating has the characteristics of the style listed there. To change this, scroll down the list until the style you wish to base the new one on is highlighted, and press Enter.

The Preview window in the Modify Style dialog box adjusts to show the different style.

5 Choose (and hold) the **F**ormat pop-up button. A pull-down list offers the various formatting options. Choose any of these options to bring up a corresponding dialog box.

Option	In the Dialog
Font	Specify any character formats and line spacings for the style. For more information, see *Font*.
Paragraph	Specify any paragraph formats for the style. For more information, see *Format Paragraph*.
Tabs	Specify any tab settings for the style. For more information, see *Tabs*.
Border	Specify any borders, boxes, and shading or shadows for the style. For more information, see *Format Borders and Shading*.
Language	Specify the language to be used in a multilingual document.
Frame	Specify any frame type, text wrap, frame size, and horizontal and vertical positioning for the frame in the style. For more information, see *Frames*.

continues

Option	In the Dialog
Numbering	A bulleted list or numbered list style can be defined (see *Bullets* for more details).

6 Make sure your style is named the way you want it.

7 Choose the OK button or press Enter to close the Style dialog box and return to the document. Your new style will be available to the document.

To apply a style

1 Position the insertion point at the beginning of the document. To apply a style to a paragraph or section of text, select the text.

2 Choose the Format Style command.

The Style dialog box appears.

3 Choose the Apply button to apply the style and return to the document.

Shortcut

Select the text you want to format, or place the insertion point at the beginning of the document, pull down the Style list on the Formatting toolbar and select the style.

Reminder

Styles can be based on other styles, such as Normal. If you change a style that *another* style or a large group of styles is based upon, they will change as well.

See also *Format Borders and Shading, Font, Format Paragraph, Frames, Tabs, Toolbar,* and *Templates.*

Style Gallery

The Style Gallery provides a list of document templates and a preview screen for viewing how those templates appear. Document templates should not be confused with styles—each template is a group of styles which are applied to a document to produce a certain effect. Templates are used with new documents to create reports, business letters, and other documents with a uniform, reliable appearance.

To start and use the Style Gallery

1 Choose the Format Style Gallery command.

The Style Gallery appears. A Template list is shown to the left, and a Preview screen displays text which shows changes as document templates are previewed.

2 Choose from the following display options:

Document	Displays the effects of a template on the current document.
Example	Displays the effects of a template on a Word sample document.
Style Samples	Displays the outline of a document template.
Browse	Choosing this button allows you to load template sets from another drive or directory.

3 When finished, choose OK or press Enter.

Summary Info

The Summary Info feature displays various items of information about the current document, including the title, subject, and author of the document; document statistics, and other information.

To access summary information

Choose the File Summary Info command.

The Summary Info dialog box appears, displaying information such as:

File Name	File name of the current document.
Directory	The directory location of the current document.
Title	The title at the top of the document.
Subject	The assigned subject of the document, if any.
Author	The Author of the document.
Keywords	Any password-protection keywords which are attached to the document.
Comments	User-editable comments attached to the document.

To view document statistics

1 Choose the File Summary Info command.
   The Summary Info dialog box appears.

2 Choose the Statistics option button.

   The Document Statistics dialog box appears.
   It displays a substantial amount of information about your document, including word and line counts, number of characters, the size of the file, the time it was last saved, the date it was created, and more. See also *Word Count*.

3 Click the Close button.

4 Choose OK or press Enter to return to the document.

Table of Authorities

Table of Authorities is a highly specialized feature which allows you to set up a legal document with a complete list of legal sources. Legal documentation is extremely voluminous in scope, and legal research requires the meticulous attribution of sources in a specific format. Word's Table of Authorities feature enables you to corroborate and refer to legal references in an efficient way.

In a legal document, legal cases are referred to as citations. Citations of cases must be selected for inclusion in a Table of Authorities. In legal documents, a case can be referred to multiple times. The first reference to a legal authority is called the *long reference*; it is the long reference which you must select for inclusion in your Table. Long citations are used only once in legal documents. All other references to legal authorities beyond the first (long) one are called *short* references.

The complete process of setting up a legal document is beyond the scope of this book. The basic Table of Authorities procedures are described below.

To select legal citations for a Table of Authorities

1 Locate the place in your document of the first "long" legal citation to include in the Table.

2 Select the text of the citation.

3 Press the key combination Alt+Shift+I.

The Mark Citation dialog box appears. The Selected Text box displays the text of the long citation.

4 Format the text as you wish it to appear in the table.

> **Tip**
>
> Only formatting shortcut keys, such as Ctrl+I, Ctrl+B, and Ctrl+U, can be employed to format text. It's more effective to generate the table after all your references are selected, and to then use your preferred styles upon it as you would any other document. Also, make sure to delete punctuation marks at the end of your selected citation.

5 The Short Citation box allows you to enter the text of the short citations you want to search for. They should be citations of the same reference as in the long reference.

6 To mark a citation, select the **M**ark option button. To mark all citations, long and short, choose the Mark **A**ll option button.

7 The next legal citation in the document can be found by choosing the **N**ext Citation button.

8 You can select the citation text in the document while the Mark Citation dialog box is still displayed. Then repeat steps 4 through 7 until all your legal references are properly marked.

9 When finished marking citations, choose the Close button.

To create a table

1 Position the insertion point where you want the table to begin.

2 Choose the Insert Index and Tables command.

3 Choose the Table of Authorities tab.

A list of available Formats is shown on the left side of the dialog box:

> Classic
>
> Elegant
>
> Formal

Simple

Custom Style

Any of the formats can be applied to the Table of Authorities you're about to generate. The following check box options are also offered:

Use **P**assim	Enables or disables use of the *passim* notation in the Table.
Keep Original Formatting	Use original text formatting of the entry.
Category	Specifies the legal references to use.
Ta**b** Leader	Enables use of a tab leader between the TOC entry and the page number.

4 The Mar**k** Citation dialog box is used to specify the first (long) legal authority reference, and to label all subsequent "short" references to the same authority. Each citation mark is used in the generation of the Table.

5 Choose OK or press Enter to generate the Table.

Table of Contents

Word 6 offers powerful features for generating tables of contents for a document.

Tables of Contents (TOCs) can be built directly from styles applied in your document. If you use several heading levels from your style list, Word will build a Table of Contents directly from them.

To mark table of contents entries with a heading style

1 Select the first item you want to include in the table of contents.

2 Choose a heading style from the Formatting Toolbar's Style list. They're numbered 1 through 9 in the standard style list.

3 Repeat steps 1 and 2 to apply heading styles to each item you want to include in the table of contents.

To mark TOC entries with fields instead of heading styles

Fields must be used in cases where obvious headings are not used in a document. Unfortunately, fields for TOC creation must be entered manually.

1 Place the insertion point immediately *after* the text you want in the TOC.

2 Press Ctrl+F9 to insert a field. A pair of curly brackets ({}) will appear.

3 Place the insertion point inside the brackets.

4 Type **TC "text"** where "text" represents the intended TOC entry—such as {TC "Chapter 1"}. Make sure the double quotes are used.

5 If intended text is to be a subentry, type in a **\L**, followed by a space, followed by the sublevel number: For example, if you have "Chapter 1" as an entry, and a second-level subentry such as "Knaves and fools," the field should read {"Knaves and fools"\L2}. The entry will be indented one level to the right of the previous entry. A third-level entry will read \L3, and so on.

6 Repeat steps 1 through 5 for each TOC entry.

7 When you finish, place the insertion point at the beginning of the document and generate the TOC by following the steps below.

To generate a table of contents

1 Mark the table of contents entries in the document.

2 Position the insertion point at the beginning of the document by pressing Ctrl+Home.

3 Choose the Insert Index and Tables command.

4 Any of the formats can be applied to the Table of Contents you're about to generate. The following check box options are also offered:

Formats	Classic, Elegant, Fancy, Modern, Formal, Simple, Custom Style
Show Page Numbers	Enables or disables the showing of page numbers in a TOC.
Right Align Page Numbers	Enables or disables alignment of page numbers with the right margin.
Show Levels	Enables or disables showing of all levels of the TOC.
Tab Leader	Enables use of a tab leader between the TOC entry and the page number.

To build a TOC from your own styles

You can also build TOC types using your own styles from the current document.

1 Choose the Insert Index and Tables command.

2 Choose the Options button.

The Table of Contents Options dialog box appears. Tables of Contents are made up of several levels and sublevels of entries, which are indented according to their sublevel. Each of the possible levels available for a TOC can have a style attached to it. Nine levels are possible.

The key is the TOC Level text box. It's a scrollable list of entry boxes, each one of which corresponds to exactly one of the styles in your document template, which are listed underneath Available Styles.

3 Enter any of the TOC levels (Level 1, Level 2, etc.) in the TOC Level text box next to the desired style, by typing a **1**, **2**, or other heading level number. Do this for all heading levels desired.

> **Tip**
>
> You can also **Reset** the list to delete all
> current TOC level entries.

4 Choose OK or press Enter to set the options, or
Cancel to avoid the changes.

5 Choose OK or press Enter to generate the table of
contents.

> **Tip**
>
> When a Table of Contents is generated, its
> text can be formatted and styles can be
> applied to it if the formats available in the
> table generation feature aren't what you're
> looking for.

See also *Index*.

Table of Figures

Tables of Figures are created in much the same way as
Tables of Contents and Authorities. Their purpose is
to create a list of illustrations in your document, for
inclusion with or separate from a table of contents.

To create entries for a table of figures

1 Position the insertion point just below the first
illustration intended for the Table.

2 Choose the Insert Caption command.

3 After typing in the caption name and setting the
options, such as caption numbering, choose OK or
press Enter (see *Captions* for more information).

To create a table of figures

1 Position the insertion point where you want the
table to begin.

2 Choose the Table Insert Table command.

The Index and Tables dialog box appears.

3 Choose the Table of Figures tab, and the Table of Figures folder appears.

4 The Preview window in the center shows a sample table of figures using the current format settings.

5 Choose an option from the Caption Labels:

Equation

Figure

Slide

Table

Choosing any one of these list options will change the contents of the Table, and the Preview visually shows the changes.

6 Choose an option from the list of Formats in the bottom left side of the dialog box:

Classic

Elegant

Fancy

Formal

Simple

Custom Style

Any of the formats can be applied to the Table of Figures you're about to generate. You can also choose from the following check box options:

Show Page Numbers	Enables or disables the showing of page numbers in a TOF.
Right Align Page Numbers	Enables or disables alignment of page numbers with the right margin.

Include Label and Number	Enables or disables showing of all levels of the TOF.
Tab Leader	Enables use of a tab leader between the TOC entry and the page number

7 You can also build Table of Figures using your own styles from the current document. To do this, select the Options button.

The Table of Figures Options dialog box appears.

8 The Build Table of Figures From check box options are as follows:

Style	Enables or disables use of a chosen style to format a Table of Figures.
Table Entry Fields	Uses the table entry fields hand-entered into the document. See below for instructions on how to enter entry fields into your document for a Table of Figures.

If you want to use a style to format a Table of Figures, select the Style, and scroll through the style list until you find the one you want. (It should be the style you may have used to format your captions.)

9 Choose OK or press Enter to set the options, or Cancel to avoid the changes.

10 Choose OK or press Enter to generate the table of figures. Word will automatically detect the captions for your table.

To insert table entry fields for a Table of Figures

1 Place the insertion point just after the caption you wish to include in the TOF.

2 Press Ctrl+F9 to insert a field. A pair of curly brackets ({}) will appear.

3 Place the insertion point inside the brackets.

4 Type in **TC "text"** where "text" represents the caption text—such as {TC "Figure 1—Marilyn Monroe"}.

Follow the end quote with a \F, as in {"Figure 1—Marilyn Monroe"\F}.

You must also place a list identifier after the \F for each entry field, such as Graph, Figure, Chart, or other explicit indicator. If you're building a list of graphs, your entry might look like:

{"Figure 1—Marilyn Monroe"\F Graph}.

Each type of illustration should have its own identifier.

5 Follow steps 1 through 4 for all of the desired figures in the document.

Also see *Captions*.

Tables

The Tables feature sets up tables so that you can organize items by columns and rows without calculating tab settings.

To create a table

1 Position the insertion point where you want the table to begin.

2 Choose the Table Insert Table command.

The Insert Table dialog box appears.

3 Type the number of columns for the table in the Number of Columns text box and the number of rows for the table in the Number of Rows text box.

4 To specify the width of the columns, type the column width in the Column Width text box or click the up or down arrow to increase or decrease the width.

5 Choose OK or press Enter to accept your choices and return to the document.

The table appears in the document.

6 Type the information into the table. Press tab to move to the next cell in the row (or from the *last* cell in a row to the *first* cell in the *next* row).

> ### Shortcut
>
> You can use a Table Wizard to quickly create a custom table of several different formats. To access the Table Wizard, choose the Table Insert Table command and choose the Wizard button.

> ### Shortcut
>
> The fastest way to create a table is to click the Table button on the standard toolbar and then drag the mouse over the table grid to select as many rows and columns as you want to include in the table. Using the Wizard allows fast creation of a more sophisticated table.

To turn table gridlines on or off

1 Select the table by dragging the mouse down the left margin of the table while holding down the left button.

2 Choose the Table Gridlines command to turn on or off the gridlines.

To insert a column or row

1 Select the column or row where you want the new column or row to appear (the selected column or row and the columns or rows that follow will move).

> ### Tip
>
> To insert more than one column or row, select the same number of columns or rows as you want to insert.

2 Choose the Table Insert Columns command or the Table Insert Rows command.

To delete a column or row in a table

1 Select the column(s) or row(s) you want to delete.

2 To delete a column, select the Table Delete Columns command. To delete a row, select the Table Delete Rows command.

To merge cells

1 Select the cells you want to merge (to combine into a single cell).

2 Choose the Table Merge Cells command.

To split a table

1 Position the insertion point where you want to split the table.

2 Choose the Table Split Table command.

A blank row appears above the current row in the table, creating a separate table.

Tabs

Word 6 offers a precise and simple method for setting left, center, right, decimal, and dotted leader tabs.

To set or change tabs

1 Position the insertion point where you want to begin using the tabs or select the paragraph(s) for which you want to set tabs.

2 Choose the Format Tabs command.

The Tabs dialog box appears.

3 To set all new tabs, choose the Clear All button. To change a specific tab, type the tab's position in the Tab Stop Position text box and then select the Clear button.

4 Type the new tab position in the **T**ab Stop Position text box or select a tab position from the list.

5 From the Alignment list box, select **L**eft, **C**enter, **R**ight, **D**ecimal, or **B**ar.

6 From the Leader list box, select **1** for None (no dot leaders), **2** for a dotted line, **3** for a dashed line, and **4** for a solid line.

7 Choose the **S**et button.

8 Repeat steps 4-7 for as many tabs as you want to set.

Note: Word for Windows has default tabs at half-inch intervals from the left margin. To return to the default tabs, select the Clear *A*ll button in the Tabs dialog box.

9 Choose OK or press Enter to confirm the tabs and return to the document.

See also *Ruler*.

Templates

Word 6 has powerful template creation features that provide patterns for shaping a document. A document template can contain boilerplate text, styles, glossary items, macros, a menu, key, and Toolbar assignments. You can use templates to standardize types of document that you use frequently.

To create a template

1 Choose the **F**ile **N**ew command.

The New dialog box appears.

2 Choose the **T**emplate option button.

3 From the **T**emplate list box, select an existing template on which you want to base the new template.

or

Select a Template Wizard from the same list which will allow you to create, in several easy steps, a custom document template.

4 Double-click the template you wish to use, and select OK or press Enter. The new document will appear with the template applied. If you start up a Wizard, you'll go through a template design, with the Wizard prompting you at each step.

5 Enter the text you want to include in the template. You can create styles, macros, glossary entries, and assign commands to a menu, key, or the Toolbar.

6 Choose the File Save As command.

7 Type a name for the new template. A template name can have up to 8 characters and cannot include spaces. (You can save a file as a document or as a template.)

Caution!

Do *not* include a file extension in the name.

8 Choose OK or press Enter to save the template.

To use a template

1 Choose the File New command.

The New dialog box appears. Template names appear in the Use Template list box.

2 Type or select the name of the template you want to use.

3 Choose OK or press Enter to use the template in the document.

Every document can have a template. If you create a document without using a template, Word for Windows uses the NORMAL.DOT template, which contains the standard document settings. Word for Windows 6 also provides a substantial set of document templates that you can use at any time.

See also *Glossary*, *Macros*, *Styles*, *Style Gallery*, and *Toolbar*.

Thesaurus

Word's Thesaurus looks up synonyms and antonyms without leaving the document.

To use the Thesaurus

1 Select the word for which you want to find synonyms or antonyms.

2 Choose the Tools Thesaurus command or press Shift+F7.

The Thesaurus dialog box appears. Suggested synonyms appear in the **S**ynonyms list box.

3 To display synonyms that have different meanings, select a different meaning from the **M**eanings list box.

Synonyms that have the selected meaning now appear in the **S**ynonyms list box.

4 To locate related words or antonyms, select the Related Word or Antonyms option from the **M**eanings list box. The related words appear in the Re-lated Words list box and the antonyms appear in the **A**ntonyms list box.

5 To locate other meanings and synonyms, select the **L**ookup button.

Other meanings appear in the **M**eanings list box and other synonyms appear in the **S**ynonyms list box.

6 To replace your word, select the replacement word from the Replace with **S**ynonym list box. When the word you selected appears in the Re**p**lace With text box, select the **R**eplace button.

To close the dialog box without changing the word in the document, select the Cancel button.

Displaying and Customizing Toolbars

Toolbars allow fast selection of commands, features, and facilities. Word for Windows provides a default toolbar, but you can customize the toolbar with buttons for frequently used commands, and display several toolbars at once. Buttons can now be dragged and dropped between the Customize toolbar facility and the toolbars themselves.

The default toolbar contains the following buttons:

Button	Name	Effect
	New	Creates a new document.
	Open	Opens a file.
	Save	Saves a file.
	Print	Prints a document.
	Print Preview	Starts Print Preview mode.
	Spelling	Starts the Spell Checker.
	Cut	Cuts text.
	Copy	Copies text.
	Paste	Pastes text.
	Format Painter	Copies formatting of the selected text to another location.

continues

Button	Name	Effect
	Undo	Undoes the preceding action.
	Redo	Repeats the last action.
	AutoFormat	Automatically formats a document.
	Insert Table	Inserts a Table.
	Insert Excel	Inserts a worksheet from Microsoft Excel.
	Columns	Inserts 1, 2, 3, or 4 columns as formatting on selected text.
	Drawing	Displays or hides the Drawing toolbar.
	Insert Chart	Inserts a chart or graph from Microsoft Graph.
	Show/Hide	Shows/Hides Hidden text
100%	Zoom Control	Controls the Zoom view of the document.
	Help	Starts Word 6 On-Line Help.

To display or hide toolbars

1 To display other toolbars, select the **View Toolbars** command.

The Toolbars dialog box appears, showing the following list of available toolbars:

Standard

Formatting

Borders

Database

Drawing

Forms

Microsoft

Word for Windows 2.0

2 Select the Toolbars you want to display. Toolbars which are checked will be displayed.

3 Use the Color Buttons and Large Buttons check box options to change the look of your toolbars.

4 Choose OK or press Enter.

To create a new toolbar

1 Choose the View Toolbars command.

The Toolbars dialog box appears.

2 Choose the New option button.

The New Toolbar dialog box appears.

3 Type in the name for the new toolbar and press Enter.

The new toolbar will be added to the list in the Toolbars dialog box.

To add and delete a button from the toolbar

1 Choose the Tools Customize command.

2 Choose the Toolbars folder.

3 From the Categories list box, select the menu or command category containing the button you want to delete. As you click on each category, the Buttons display changes to show other sets of Toolbar buttons.

4 To add a button to any toolbar displayed in the Word 6 screen, select the desired button and hold down the mouse. Drag the button over to the toolbar on the Word screen.

Shortcut

Buttons can also be dragged from the
Customize Toolbar dialog box, or from a
toolbar, to the desktop.

5 To delete the button from the toolbar, do the oppo-
site: drag a button off the toolbar onto the Customize Toolbars dialog box. The button will be removed
from the toolbar.

6 Choose the Close button to close the dialog box.

Tip

Enabling the Show ToolTips check box in
the Toolbar dialog box will allow small captions, highlighted in yellow, to be displayed
as the mouse moves over each button. Also,
as the mouse passes over each button in a
Toolbar, the Status Bar at the bottom of the
Word 6 screen will display a description of
the button's function.

See also *Macros*.

Tools Options

The Tools Options command encompasses many of
Word 6's most important program settings. It enables
you to customize Word for Windows options.

To select the type of option to customize

1 Choose the Tools Options command.

The Options dialog box appears. Choose any of
the following 12 folders, each bearing Word for
Windows features which can be changed:

Folder	Functions
AutoFormat	Sets Automatic Formatting options.
Compatibility	Allows maximum compatibility with other word processor file formats.
Edit	Sets options such as Drag-and-Drop, Smart Cut & Paste, and other editing options.
File Locations	Sets directories where Word automatically seeks for files.
Print	Sets print controls, update fields, field codes, annotations, and hidden text.
General	Sets general options such as screen color, WordPerfect Help, and others.
Grammar	Sets styles and grammar rules for documents.
Spelling	Sets spelling rules and custom dictionaries.
User Info	Sets your name, initials, and mailing address.
View	Sets defaults for hidden text, table gridlines, and nonprinting characters.

Word for Windows displays the dialog box for the option you select.

2 For any set of options, when you're finished, choose OK or press Enter to return to your document.

Underline Text

Word's Underline feature can add emphasis to text in your document.

To use underlines

1 Select the text to underline or place the insertion point where you wish to enter underlined text.

2 Choose the underline button on the Formatting toolbar or press Ctrl+U.

> ### Tip
>
> To turn underlining off, choose the under-lining button again or press Ctrl+U again. This applies to selected text or any location of the insertion point in a document.

Undo

Word's Undo feature reverses, undoes, or undeletes the most recent change to a document.

Word for Windows 6 now offers the ability to undo multiple actions. The last action performed is the first Undo level, the next to last action is the second Undo, and so on.

Occasionally, you'll only be able to undo the last action. Be wary, and save your work consistently.

To use Undo

Choose the **E**dit **U**ndo command or press Ctrl+Z. Repeat as needed for multiple undos.

Word for Windows reverses the most recent change to the document.

User Information

The User Information feature adds basic information to the header in your document file about the author's name, initials, and mailing address.

To view and change user information

1 Choose the Tools Options command.

The Options dialog box appears.

2 Choose the User Info tab.

3 Clicking the mouse once inside the Name, Initials, or Mailing Address fields allows you to edit and change the user information in each respective field.

4 Choose OK or press Enter to save the changes, or Cancel to ignore them.

View (Viewing Document screen modes)

Word offers several different Views of your document, including normal, outline, or page layout view, among other menu options.

Views allow you to see your document from a different perspective. Page Layout view, for example, lets you view your document as it will be printed, while retaining all editing features and capabilities (unlike Print Preview). Normal View is the Word default, but does not show headers and footers, multiple columns, and other aspects of the document.

To view a document

1 Choose the View menu.

2 Choose one of the following views:

Option	Effect
Normal	Enables you to type, edit, and format a document.
Outline	Enables you to create and view the outline structure of a document and to move to a different location in the document or to copy and move text more quickly than in Normal view.
Page Layout	Displays multiple columns, headers and footers, and footnotes in the document.
Master Document	Displays the master document.
Full Screen	Enables you to type, edit, and format a document.
Zoom	Enlarges or reduces the view of a page on-screen.

3 The Toolbars and the Ruler can also be enabled or disabled from here. Header and Footer editing can also be enabled here.

See also *Outlines* and *Zoom*.

Word Count

Word Count is a handy Word feature for displaying a fast word count of your current document, without going through the Summary Info feature.

To use Word Count

1 Choose the Tools Word Count command.

Word for Windows displays counts for the following:

Pages

Words

Characters

Paragraphs

Lines

2 Choose OK or press Enter to return to the document.

Also see *Summary Info*.

Zoom

Word 6's Zoom feature enlarges or reduces the view of a page on-screen. Text on the screen can be smaller or bigger, and may show the whole page or a smaller section of it at higher magnification.

To zoom a document

1 Choose the View Zoom command.

2 Choose one of the following option buttons:

Option	Effect
Magnification	Enlarges or reduces the page. You can select 200%, 100% (default), 75%, 50%, or Custom. If you select Custom, enter a different percentage.
Page Width	Reduces wide documents to display the full width on-screen.
Whole Page	Displays an entire page on-screen.

3 Choose OK or press Enter.

> ## Shortcut
>
> You can quickly zoom to certain settings by choosing the Zoom Whole Page, Zoom 100%, or Zoom Page Width button on the Toolbar.

See also *Toolbar* and *View.*

Index